How to Be Prepared to
Think on Your Feet

How to Be Prepared to Think on Your Feet

Stephen C. Rafe

HARPER BUSINESS

A Division of Harper & Row Publishers, New York

Grand Rapids, Philadelphia, St. Louis, San Francisco
London, Singapore, Sydney, Tokyo, Toronto

International Standard Book Number: 0-88730-437-0

Library of Congress Catalog Card Number: 90-4438

Printed in the United States of America

Library of Congress Cataloging-in-Publication Data

Rafe, Stephen C.
    How to be prepared to think on your feet/Stephen C. Rafe
       p. cm.
    Includes bibliographical references
    1. Public speaking. I. Title.
    PN4121.R26 1990
    808.5′1—dc20   90-4438
                                       CIP

90 91 92 93 HC 9 8 7 6 5 4 3 2 1

To Lorena Scott,
my high school teacher who said, "I believe in you. Make something of yourself." This book is for you, as a tribute to all the caring people of this world who have reached beyond themselves with words and gestures to influence the lives of others.

Contents

Part Three: Taking Charge of Your *Situation*

Learn how environments can make or break a presentation. Find out which room arrangements best suit the way you will present your information. Consider how the time of day and day of the week can affect your audience's receptivity. Get the best from such "tools" as lecterns, microphones, easels, blackboards, and projection equipment.

Acknowledgments

The empathy, compassion, and encouragement of two special people helped make the development of this book a pleasure:

Virginia Smith, my executive editor, is a patient, caring, and constructive professional. Her support throughout the editing process enabled us to turn a collection of workshop notes, lectures, handouts, and feature articles into a book that will help readers improve their presentation skills.

Linda Hayes, my literary agent, trusted her professional intuition well enough to agree to work with me, even though we had only met by phone, and she had not even seen a book outline. I thank her for her win-win approach to life.

Throughout my career, several people influenced my future in exceptional ways. In writing this book, I became particularly aware of the role played by John R. Hayes, Jr., who set high standards as a supervisor early in my career and then instilled within me the desire to pursue those standards.

Although clients look to their outside consultants as authorities, the clients themselves frequently contribute more to the consultants' knowledge than they may realize. Their thought-provoking questions keep me constantly searching for real explanations instead of mere answers, and I am grateful for this challenge.

I also appreciate those who have taught my clients with me over the years. Their desire to help others learn has provided an ongoing and welcomed opportunity to improve my personal teaching skills.

Years of research and constant updating have gone into this book, and I can finally extend a warm thank you to the many librarians in public and private libraries everywhere for their many courtesies over the years, courtesies that often go well beyond one's traditional sense of "duty."

To the editors and publishers of periodicals who accept my work, your willingness to run material that often borders on the fringe of current thinking is an act of trust and confidence that I will continue to appreciate as we strive to find new and better communications techniques.

As a child, it seemed that the many adults in my life took a peculiar pleasure in correcting the grammar of anyone who spoke within earshot. Only as an adult did I come to appreciate just how much their persistence would shape my career.

My wife and children have often sacrificed their own priorities, so that I could help others through my teaching, speaking, and writing. Through the enrichment of their love, they have enabled me to return that gift to them and to extend it to others.

Thank you all for caring.

Introduction

What would you do if you were a key executive in one of the largest companies in America and the speech you were scheduled to deliver tomorrow had just been transcended by the day's events?

This happened to one of my clients: He had just conducted a news teleconference on the East Coast and was scheduled to address another audience of newspeople on the West Coast the next day. During the impromptu give-and-take with reporters in the teleconference, he covered many of the points his prewritten speech called for him to address. Clearly, he would need to update his main content. He would also need a new opening and a new ending. New points introduced at the teleconference would have to be incorporated, expanded upon, and sequenced in a logical order. Material that had been used to underscore specific points during the teleconference would have to be replaced, reworked, or at least given a different emphasis.

There was no time for outlining in the traditional sense. The text would have to be typed in a way that would facilitate a cold reading. The rehearsal would have to be brief, focused on the key essentials.

He would have to push through any normal and expected post-teleconference fatigue. He would also have to overcome jet lag, lack of sleep, and the added stress of delivering a rewritten text before newspeople, many of whom had seen him on television the day before.

Within hours, the speech would have to be reorganized, rewritten, rehearsed, and delivered. It was—and thanks to the skills of an executive who represented the epitome of integrity and communications skills, it received a standing ovation.

The techniques provided in this book helped make that possible.

The same techniques have also helped thousands of other executives to prepare and deliver presentations for events ranging from fertilizer sales meetings with farmers in feed-supply warehouses to testimony before Congress.

Deciding to reveal this much of my coaching methods in a book was not easy: Clients pay me handsomely to teach them what you can now learn just by reading this book. However, some time ago I discovered that when you cast your bread on the waters, you do get back more, indeed, than soggy bread. Thus, this book holds nothing back in terms of specific, tangible guidance. It gives you everything my seminars and coaching sessions cover except those points that must still be covered in private counseling: the coaching related to your particular business, the opportunity to work on your specific issues, and the specific, individual critiques of your progress that help you bring out your personal best.

This is not a book *about* business presentations. You will find it packed with tips, tactics, and tangible advice you can use. Whether you are an experienced speaker or are about to face your first management meeting, this book will help you do even better than you might have done otherwise.

As you read, you will find some familiar ideas, others that may be new but seem so logical that you may wonder why you hadn't thought of them earlier, and still others that appear to fly in the face of conventional thinking.

My best advice is to accept them as they are. Suspend judgment, even if you feel that some ideas may not work for you, or even if you have already tried something similar without much success. It is axiomatic that much of the advice we are given in life will be of little value if: 1. We try to use it in isolation and out of context; and 2. we abandon it before we give it the opportunity to become integrated into our way of doing things.

Read this book through before trying any of its discrete techniques, and you will find that its program approach works best as a whole. Those who have tried patching bits and pieces of my methods into their own approaches over the years have frequently acknowledged later that they improved most quickly when they abandoned their previous concepts of "right" and "wrong" techniques and adopted this system in its entirety.

If you are like most people with whom I've worked, you may have found that you are comfortable speaking when you are *part* of a group, yet experience pit-of-the-stomach feelings when you have to *face* the same number of people. Perhaps you can even pinpoint one area of concern in which you would like to improve your presentations. For some, it's the personal skills area, for others the writing of the presentation, and for still others the situations themselves.

This book will give you a new way of thinking about these essentials. It will help you deal with personal concerns, develop the right presentation for your audience, and arrange the room for maximum effectiveness.

You can use the information that follows, as thousands have already done, to do more than deliver business presentations. You can apply the same principles when you need to address other internal meetings, teach at the college level, deliver government testimony, brief news organizations, and speak before any type of group.

The techniques you will discover here have been shared with clients in such organizations as Texaco, DuPont, IBM, AT&T, Johnson & Johnson, NASA, Ciba Geigy, and numerous others in political, governmental, religious, and service fields across the country and in other nations.

The book is organized into three parts:

PART ONE: TAKING CHARGE OF YOUR SELF
Bring out your personal best by improving your skills with such tools as voice dynamics, gestures and animation, eye contact, and attitude. Learn how clothing, diet, and rest can affect performance. Deal with speakers' major concern—stress—and succeed.

PART TWO: TAKING CHARGE OF YOUR SUBJECT
Follow my unique method, "Organizing Words from End to Beginning ©," which I have taught to thousands, including professional speechwriters, and you will never have to stare at a blank page again, wondering what to write. Turn raw material into manageable units. Learn how to mark a text for dynamic delivery, and how to bring your talk alive.

Discover a new way to prepare your text. Find out how to profile audiences and organizations and how to determine what will motivate them best. Consider the pros and cons of manuscripts versus note cards. Deal with interruptions in new ways. Learn how to get back on track if you suffer a memory lapse.

PART THREE: TAKING CHARGE OF YOUR SITUATION
Learn how environments can make or break a presentation, and what to do about it. Find out which room arrangements best suit the way you will present your information. Consider how even the time of day and day of the week can affect your audience's receptivity. Get the best from

such "tools" as lecterns, microphones, easels, blackboards, and projection equipment.

Research shows that adults learn best when they receive information in sequential and cumulative fashion, marking their progress from one part to the next. We have made every effort to design this book according to these principles, so that it will help you to become a better speaker. As you go through its pages, we hope you will agree.

"The two most engaging powers of an author are to make new things familiar, and familiar things new."

Samuel Johnson

Part One
Taking Charge of Your *Self*

1
Your Attitude

Through counseling private clients, I have learned that the best progress takes place only when matters of self are fully addressed, and all concerns in this area are satisfied. When I first started in this field, I often found that when I began a session by talking about information gathering, writing, or setting up a room, clients were almost totally occupied with personal concerns—usually having to do with nervousness.

For example, several years ago I was called in to coach one business executive strictly about the use of teleprompters. Since he was an experienced presenter and was on a tight schedule, I proceeded quickly beyond the social amenities (introductions, small talk about the trip and the weather) and began to talk about how teleprompters work.

Within the first five minutes, I happened to say something about a "wheelbarrow-load" of information we could cover about teleprompters, but that I would limit our session to the bare essentials. He seemed to be listening, so I continued. After giving him about five minutes of pointers, I suggested that he stand up and try reading a paragraph I had prepared in advance.

He looked puzzled and said absently, "I'm sorry, what did you want the wheelbarrow for?" Clearly, he had been preoccupied, and we had to deal with matters of self before any learning could take place. Until you learn the techniques for taking care of *you,* you may have the same kinds of experience with stress—no matter how well you have written your speech or have taken care of physical arrangements. The information that follows will help you not only with your business presentations, but also in many other aspects of your life, both professional and personal.

When I prepare people to deliver presentations and to respond to questions in all environments, I often appreciate the power of one of the world's worst fears—the fear of facing audiences. *The People's Almanac Presents The Book of Lists* by David Wallenchinsky, Irving Wallace, and Ann Wallace indicates that Americans rank this fear number one, higher than the fear of death, which they list as number seven.

If you have ever encountered the fear of facing an audience, you are familiar with its classic signs: accelerated heartbeat, lightheadedness, a "bonging" or a high-pitched sound in your head, difficulty breathing, sweating (or the other extreme, cold extremities), dryness in the throat, trembling in the jaw or other parts of your body, and possibly even the feeling of being disconnected from your body and the desire to flee.

Yet, despite all the trauma associated with the act of facing audiences, business people are increasingly called on to present their ideas and information. It is critical that they overcome their apprehension about facing audiences. The experience need not be the way a participant in one of my workshops put it. In opening the two-day session, I went around the room asking: "What would you like—more than anything else—to get out of this session?" When I got to one obviously nervous man, he responded: "Me? Just as quickly as possible. Before I pass out!"

What the Mind Conceives

Studies show that the old saying, "You are what you think you are," may be true. When we put the various parts of our bodies in certain positions, we affect how we think or feel—even if we may not be aware of it. Behavior researchers tell us that changes in our physiological state are accompanied by corresponding changes, both conscious and unconscious, in our mental-emotional state.

This principle also has a converse side. As Elmer and Alyce Green put it, "Every change in the mental-emotional state, conscious or unconscious, is accompanied by an appropriate change in the physiological state."

People must already believe that they can influence or change their emotions through physical means; otherwise, what would be the value of such expressions as "settle down," "stand tall," or "watch yourself?" A statement such as, "Stop acting so nervous," also indicates that we believe we can exercise some control over the physical aspects of an emotion, if not the emotion itself.

Take fear, nervousness, or apprehension, for example. When we find ourselves experiencing one of those feelings, the body tends to adapt its functions accordingly. Muscles tense, heartbeat quickens, blood surges, faces flush, and so on. Both involuntary and voluntary organs and muscles are activated. In a new situation, the stimulation may be particularly strong.

Scientists tell us that this is one of the ways we protect ourselves from anything that might threaten, or appear to threaten, us. It is part of our natural drive toward self-preservation. The key to managing it lies in our ability to change our mind's perceptions of what is threatening and what is not.

What Emotions Look Like

Every emotion has its corresponding physical counterparts. For example, you know what a defeated athlete is "supposed" to look like. You also know the postures and gestures of an angry person, or of a customer who has been kept waiting too long.

In fact, if you have ever found yourself in a situation where you felt that strong non-verbal actions were necessary, you may have even tried a little harder to get that mood, that point, across. As you did, you probably felt yourself actually attuning your thoughts more to your postures. The more you "acted" angry, the more angry you may have actually felt.

This shows that the brain can take on the emotions that are appropriate to the postures you may be exhibiting. As Anthony Robbins says in his book, *Unlimited Power,* "Physiology is the lever to emotional change."

He says that although we think of depression, for example, as an emotional state, it is clearly identified by physical postures. He says, "Depressed people often walk around with their eyes down. They drop their shoulders. They take weak, shallow breaths."

To help alleviate depression, a good first step would be to assume the opposite postures: Raise the head, stand erect, square the shoulders, and breathe deeply and rhythmically. This would send an entirely different message to the brain—one of confidence. The same approach can be used even more effectively when dealing with the lesser emotions, such as the stress commonly associated with business presentations.

Change the State

If you don't like the behavior that results from your physical (and emotional) state, change the state. If you don't think you can change your feelings, change the postures and actions that accompany the feelings. Your mind should follow this lead. So says Paul Ekman, of the Human Interaction Laboratory, Langley Porter Institute in San Francisco.

Dr. Ekman says that we become what we put on our faces (and the rest of our bodies). He advises, for instance, that if you want to have a good feeling, smile or laugh, even though you may not feel like doing so, and soon your attitude will change. He says that the physical act triggers biological processes, such as increased blood flow and oxygen to the brain. These are then relayed through neurotransmitters to alter the mind's perception of what it is "supposed to" feel.

A while back, a high-ranking executive of a leading automobile manufacturer asked me to help him with the way he ran meetings. People did not like his style. When I asked him what he thought his major drawback might be, he simply said, "I don't smile."

"Never?" I asked him, noting that he had returned my smile when we first met and had smiled several other times as we had coffee together while laying out the morning's program.

"Never," he replied.

"Okay," I responded, deferring all other possibilities for the moment. After a few more minutes of conversation, he was ready to show me how he might open a typical meeting.

We videotaped this, and, as he predicted, he didn't smile. When he concluded this segment, I said "Cut," but allowed the camera to keep rolling.

Unaware of this, he looked at me and said—with a big grin—"See. I told you. I don't smile."

We played back the brief tape immediately. Just as he thought we had ended, he saw his big smile on the screen. I pressed the pause button to hold his expression on screen and looked at him.

"You son-of-a-gun," he said with a chuckle, "you did that."

"Yup," I responded, conveying both mock mischief and encouragement with my voice. "And see how good it looks."

We talked about that and about what he was feeling when he smiled and when he looked at his own smiling face on the monitor. We then went right into another taping in which he agreed to try to smile a little earlier. A twinkle was evident almost from the start, and when the smile came, it was a bit strained at first, then suddenly became very warm.

During the critique, he told me that when he practiced the opening that time, he found himself chuckling inside at having been "caught" smiling. He agreed that it felt "pretty good." Three more tapings and his smile was natural and friendly. He mentioned that he had been concerned earlier about whether smiling might make him seem less dignified or authoritative. On the contrary, he concluded, he'd "rather buy a used car" from an executive who allowed the warmth of a smile to come through than from one who didn't, and he now felt much better smiling than not smiling.

The change was not a pivotal point in a career, but it shows how body language and emotions go hand in hand.

The Roots of Emotions

The word "emotion," itself, points to the connection between mind and body. The prefix "e" means from or after, and the suffix "motion" means movement.

Every emotion needs a cause or a trigger—something sensory that stimulates the mind to respond. It may be a new situation, or it may be one that the mind has experienced in the past. The response is expressed in physical changes that affect both mind and body.

To demonstrate this for yourself, think about squeezing a lemon and dripping the juice into your mouth. Did you just salivate? Yet, there was no lemon, just your thoughts of one. Now, if you can cause saliva to flow by thought alone, you can certainly do the reverse and change thought through physical actions.

To prove the point to yourself, think of something that "gives you the chills." Is it the sound of fingernails or chalk being squeaked on a blackboard? Could it be the feeling of a fork or the stick from an ice cream bar being dragged through your teeth? Or the sound of two pieces of styrofoam scraping against each other?

Once your mind recalls that image, sound, or feeling, your body is likely to develop goose bumps, or do whatever it does when you "get the chills."

However, if your mind can generate *that* response to *that* stimulus, it can also learn to respond more appropriately to other stimuli. In effect, when it is no longer useful for you to feel nervous before facing an audience, you will stop being nervous. You can change your emotional responses to situations by the way you think about them and act in their presence. Fear is only a response of the body's systems to whatever stimulated that emotion.

We know we can control our emotions by controlling the physical ways in which we express them. Although the concept may seem new, much of this knowledge is ancient. A Greek philosopher named Epictetus said that it is not events themselves that trouble us, but rather our perception of them. The Bible tells us, "As a man thinketh, so is he." In more recent times, in the late nineteenth century, William James, one of the founders of psychology in the United States, investigated the connection between emotions and physical processes. He concluded that emotions "die" when one takes away the body language associated with them.

So the next time you need to communicate confidence and your mind is buzzing with messages of insecurity, assume more appropriate physical postures and breathing, and allow your thoughts to follow along. You might not sell the idea, get the promotion, or persuade the boss, but you'll do a better job at presenting, and you'll be better able to handle whatever response you receive.

Using "Self-talk" Constructively

When you prepare to face an audience, your attitude and "self-talk" can determine your success. Think positive thoughts to have a positive outcome.

As you consider your next presentation, you must constantly reaffirm your ability to succeed. For example, when you feel nervous, you should think about feeling calm. You should not even say the word "nervous" to yourself. If you were to say "I'm *NOT* nervous," for example, your subconscious mind would still hear and record the word "nervous." Instead, think CALM and POSITIVE thoughts, such as, "I am calm. My presentation contains many important points that I am pleased to share. I know I can deliver it well."

Remember that audiences want you to succeed. They are there to hear whatever you can offer them. You are there to help them, to share information with them.

Understanding Personalities

When we deal with people, most of us devote a lot of our subconscious—and even conscious—attention to "sizing up" others: We try to use criteria from past experiences to help us evaluate them in terms of ourselves. "Will I like them?" and "Will they like me?" are basic questions. You may be using even more sophisticated ones in your own sorting process—questions that you may not even have been aware of on a conscious level.

Presenters quickly need to make sense of their relationships with their audience members—in particular, in terms that are relevant to the participants' acceptance of the information presented. An astute speaker can assess this through non-verbal cues even before benefiting from the additional input that questions and comments from the audience members provide.

Many of my clients have discussed the experience of having been in the middle of making a point when they noticed that someone suddenly looked "annoyed," or had just tuned them out. Often, they said, they didn't know what to do about what they saw, and sometimes even lost their place in their presentation, or felt their confidence slip.

Most of them said they went on speaking and tried to "hook" such individuals back into the process. In some cases, they felt they had succeeded. In others, they felt they did not, but made a further effort during the Q&A period to find out why. Even there, some succeeded, and some didn't.

However, in every case, the issue at hand had become emotionally involving to the presenter. What they had missed was that the participants' messages reflected their own feelings, often separate and apart from anything the presenters may have done or said. This is most often the case.

Nonetheless, you need a sorting tool that you can use quickly to determine audience members' temperaments or dispositions at a given moment. I examined personality tests and explored many models of human personality to devise such a useful tool. One helpful model was developed by researcher Tim LaHaye and is based on observations that go back to Hippocrates and were further refined by a Greek philosopher and physician named Galen early in the second century A.D. It delineates four temperaments: sanguine, choleric, melancholy, and phlegmatic.

In the LaHaye model, sanguines and cholerics tend to be externally oriented, facing outward and displaying more concern for others. Melancholies and phlegmatics tend to be internally oriented, facing inward and showing more concern for self.

The Rafe Model

I have adapted that four-temperament theory and modified it to build on knowledge of the polarities of approach and avoidance behavior. It consists of Approach I, Approach II, Avoidance I, and Avoidance II temperaments. Executives find it simple to learn and easy to use—even under fire.

For quick reference:

- Approach I—Words, voice tones, and body language combine to say, "I want to approach you." (Active–Gregarious)
- Approach II—Words, voice tones, and body language combine to say, "I would accept an approach from you to me." (Passive–Reticent but friendly)
- Avoidance I—Words, voice tones, and body language combine to say, "I want to keep you away from me." (Active–Hostile, aggressive)
- Avoidance II—Words, voice tones, and body language combine to say, "I want to keep me away from you." (Passive–Fearful, insecure)

All people contain varying elements of these four types, with one type generally predominating in any given situation. When you can size up a questioner's mode when he or she asks a question, you will have an edge in coming up with a response that will satisfy everyone.

Here's how to use the technique: Let's say you are in a meeting, and someone in the group asks you a question. Observe her word choices, voice tones, and non-verbal signals as you ask yourself:

- Is she trying to approach me or avoid me?
- If you decide she is using avoidance behavior, ask yourself whether she is trying to:

1. keep you away from her ("pushing" you away), or
2. keep herself away from you (withdrawing or retreating).

If she appears to be using approach behavior, ask yourself whether she is indicating that she is:

1. clearly outgoing, or
2. approachable.

Recognize that you are processing these impressions through your own personal biases and that you may be misreading others' signals, or calibrating them incorrectly. At best, you are only forming a temporary assessment of the person's behavior, so that you can explore the best way to achieve rapport. You may need additional input before you can confirm your initial observations.

Of the four personality types, most audiences (though only while they are an audience) are likely to be Approach II. They are generally relaxed, patient, and in control. Usually, they are amiable and receptive to new information. They will welcome any interest you show in them, or in their needs and interests. They will appreciate any efforts you make to tailor your comments to them, specifically. They will also be receptive to new information that will help them without placing them at risk.

Of course, as individuals, some audience members may have a stronger need than others to hear bottom-line results (Avoidance I). So if you anticipate having several Avoidance I types among your participants, you will at least have to allude early in your presentation to the outcome you intend to present.

Some participants may want proof and guarantees (Avoidance II). You can address their needs as you go along by providing proof, through supporting information, and by offering guarantees in your conclusion.

Still other participants may expect to hear testimonials (Approach I). Let them know throughout your text who supports your statements, or quote recognizable names as sources.

Of course, if you can address the needs of all three types—"something for everyone" as the saying goes—you will increase the likelihood of having them accept your message. Knowing this much about your participants will give you a good start when you consider how to frame your content as you write your presentation.

Behavior is often situational: The same person might communicate in an entirely different way on another issue or topic, at another meeting, or in other circumstances. Also, the intensity of others' signals may vary according to their stake in the outcome of the discussion. So, use your initial input only to check approach/avoidance behavior and to determine whether it is active or passive.

When you have concluded that an individual is displaying avoidance behavior, you should ask yourself:

- What might lie behind the behavior I appear to be observing?
- Does this person feel offended? Ignored? Treated poorly? Put off? Given the runaround?
- Does she have a specific need? Might it be to impress, to persuade, or to be treated well?
- Are there other possibilities?

As you speak with a person who displays any of the four modes, be sure you ask the questions that will give you the input you need to prevent mind-reading. Avoid concluding early that you know what is actually going on, or that you know what the other person is thinking or trying to do. Often, these presumptions don't check out later.

Instead, postpone judgmental or defensive thinking, keep your own feelings away from difficult matters, and strive to understand others better. This will help you allow for the possibility that others are well-intentioned. That's a major step toward achieving better outcomes in your efforts to communicate.

A QUICK "HOW TO"

First, we might recognize our own judgmental thoughts. Those such as, "She's trying to give me a hard time," or "He's not going to dump that one on me," occur often. Yet, think of how much better you would feel immediately if you could ask yourself instead: "What behavior is this person displaying?"

When you believe that someone is in an Avoidance mode, stay calm and try to listen to how this is expressed:

- Is she attacking others? If so, is she doing this by minimizing (damning with faint praise), by teasing (either ridicule or sarcasm), or by gossiping? By asking specific questions, can you determine her reason for doing so?
- Is he trying to compare you unfavorably with others? What is he saying, and why is he saying it?
- Is she making demands of you or of others? What are her expectations? Are they reasonable? What lies behind them? Are the demands implied or clearly stated?
- Is he trying to control you, or others, or the situation? What gives you these impressions? How can you check them out? If asked, what would he say motivates his actions?

- Does her total communication (words, tones, non-verbals) indicate that she is trying to impress you by building up herself? This is a tough one because at first it might appear to be Approach I behavior ("I want you to approach, or like, me"). However, when overdone, it turns many listeners off, swinging them over to Avoidance I (pushing them away from her).

If you feel that someone is in an Approach mode, monitor how they are expressing this:

- Are they coming on strong? Are they trying to take over, or monopolize the dialogue? Are they praising you or others excessively? If so, will they yield the floor back to you when you ask for it? Can you get them to let you know what's behind their comments?
- Are they selling their own agenda? Pushing their favorite point—even in the face of clear-cut, collective disagreement?
- Do they want honesty at all costs, to "tell it like it is," leading the discussion into a kind of disclosure that would be more appropriate in another forum?
- Are they overgeneralizing, missing important details in their comments?
- Are they trying to minimize a situation, hoping that it will somehow go away without specific action being taken?
- Do they go part way in expressing their views, then back off? Are they overly deferential toward others?
- Do they appear supportive? Are they relaxed and purposeful in their style of commenting?
- Do their overall messages (words, tones, non-verbals) indicate that they are active or passive in their deportment at the moment?

Assessing Others

If you are having a dialogue, such as when you are accepting questions, listen carefully—especially for statements that seem too broad (such as "always" or "never"), judgmental (such as "should" or "must"), vague (such as "they" or "things"), and try to find out what the speaker means by those words. Ask for a clarification, or put the speaker's comments in your own terms and ask whether you have interpreted him or her correctly.

Suppose, for example an audience member were to say: "They should always use Parking Lot C." Your response might be: "Well,

Alexis, if I understand you correctly, you believe that by having workers on the third shift park in lot C, we might eliminate some of the jams in lot B during the shift changes. Is that correct?"

Generally, Avoidance I individuals will respond best to someone who is well-prepared and gets right to the bottom line, supporting his or her arguments with specifics. They prefer agreement with their views to disagreement and will respond best to people who draw them to acceptable conclusions rather than telling them what to do.

Avoidance II people also like proof or documentation and the weight of evidence. However, they are less impatient and will welcome a discussion of the pros and cons of any important issue. They like schedules, plans of action, and low-risk situations.

Approach I individuals tend to be more responsive to the views or testimonials of others—particularly people whom they consider authorities. They will respond best when you present information in a friendly and entertaining way, and without a lot of details.

Approach II people are generally the most accepting of the four types. Your challenge will be to encourage them to participate, to draw them out, and to "defend" them against the Avoidance I and Approach I people, in particular. Like the Avoidance II individuals, they, too, will be most responsive when you present specific solutions that offer as little risk taking as possible.

Stay in Charge of YOU

Remember that you are always in charge of your own responses. No one can cause you to say things you don't choose to say, or have emotions you don't choose to have.

If the situation is especially difficult, you will generally cope better when you can hold a thought, such as one of these, in mind:

- No matter what is happening, or might happen, I will not let it affect me personally.
- I accept myself and this individual, and I make no judgments. I merely observe both my behavior of the moment, and theirs.
- I am doing my best to do what I feel is right, and this individual is entitled to the same presumption.
- I will remain calm and not make hasty judgments. This will help me feel better about both the situation and myself, now and later.
- Over time, my patience and understanding will be rewarded and may even pay immediate dividends.

With one or more of these thoughts in mind, it becomes easier to empathize with all four types of personalities. Regardless of their behavior at the moment, you will then be better able to respond to them with such statements as these: "I can understand your feelings," or "From your perspective, that would make sense to me," or "Let's see how we can resolve this."

Creating a Better Rapport

In your internal meetings (and even in those outside your organization), the following techniques can help you establish a better rapport with any individual—especially with those who are being "difficult":

You can match their verbs (visual, auditory, or kinesthetic), so that you are sending information in the same mode in which they are processing it. You can also match their rate of speech. A fast-speaking person is generally processing information in the visual mode. A moderate-speaking rate usually indicates the auditory mode. Slow rates of speech generally indicate a tactile mode. You can also match a person's voice tones, pitch, intensity, and inflections.

As you listen to anyone who either takes the initiative or responds to your invitation to ask questions, monitor what you are thinking, what your mind is saying to itself. This self-talk is three times faster than verbal conversation, and the conscious mind tends to believe what the subconscious mind tells it.

So, if you say, "This person is making me angry," your subconscious will respond accordingly. Even, "I'm not going to get angry" is not good because "angry" still reaches your subconscious. Instead, concentrate your thoughts on something such as, "I will remain calm," or "This person's attitude reminds me to remain understanding."

Relieving Stress Further

When you deal with difficult people, breathe evenly and keep your body free of stress and tension. Release tension spots discreetly. When you are speaking, purposeful gesturing will help.

As we have discussed, stress is simply your mind's way of trying to help you deal constructively with whatever is confronting you. Just change your mind about how you choose to feel. You are, indeed, in charge of your emotions.

Smile a pleasant, understanding smile—not a smirk or a grimace—

even if you're not happy about what is going on. Smiling is another way to tell the mind that you are in charge of your feelings and that it can stop pumping you up for action.

Finally, when the situation ends, as all situations must at some point, think to yourself: "It's over. I did my best. Let me put this aside and get on with my life."

This will help release any residual stress felt when dealing with difficult people. It will also help you get ready for the next dialogue—which may be very positive, indeed.

2
Stress Relief

The best speech-writing and delivery techniques in the world are of little use to someone who has not been able to overcome his or her feelings of stress and anxiety when facing audiences. You will deal far more effectively with this universal problem once you follow the advice outlined in this chapter.

The methods presented here have provided almost instant relief for many of my clients. In fact, in several cases they have used them successfully as I worked with them just minutes before facing major audiences.

Obviously, you must have something to offer, and your audience must have something to gain, otherwise they would have scheduled another speaker—or stayed home. Nonetheless, stress and nerves are realities that all speakers must face.

Just as you can't have water without hydrogen and oxygen, you can't have emotions without both physical and mental aspects. This sounds logical enough, and it is.

Stage Fright as a Skill

The act of developing a specific emotion in response to a specific stimulus or situation can actually be called a skill because it requires knowing when to have the feelings, how to have the feelings (including body posture), and how intense the feelings "need" to be. Regarded as a skill, even a fear, such as stage fright, is learned (sometimes with the first exposure to the stimulus).

The mind is constantly alert to anything that might threaten or appear to threaten it, and it stimulates chemicals that help the body act toward its own survival. This drive toward self-preservation is called the fight/flight syndrome.

The individual's mind and body prepare him or her to fight or run when subjected to certain stimuli. In a new situation, the stimulation may be particularly strong.

Before you address an audience, you face an added problem: You cannot fight or run. You must endure the emotion. You will either overcome the feelings and grow more comfortable before audiences, or you will intensify your nervous emotions further and have even more anxiety facing audiences in the future.

If the latter happens, you actually practice ("learning") having the feelings of stage fright. This includes knowing when to have them, where to have them, and how to have them. From that viewpoint, stage fright may actually be a skill.

Calming Body and Mind

Here's the good news: If you can learn something, you can also "unlearn" it. Psychologists have demonstrated this over the decades. They have shown that any emotion that can be triggered by a given stimulus can also be extinguished or gotten rid of—particularly when it is replaced by a more useful response to the same situation. Behaviorists refer to this as "counter-conditioning."

For example, if a situation makes you feel tense, such as when you face audiences, the counter behavior would be to learn to relax whenever you're in that environment. You can do this through another behavior-shaping technique called "systematic desensitization."

For example, when a person fears water, the fear should be overcome gradually. Start by learning to enjoy being near water. Next, learn to like being in shallow water. Then, gradually increase the depth.

Desensitization alone, however, is not enough. You should also replace the fear of water with a new emotion that can compete successfully with it, for instance, the good feeling of being able to swim.

The same logic holds true for stage fright: Ideally, you should start by learning to be comfortable entering rooms where speeches might be given. Then, you should practice staying in the room for increasing periods—each time gradually moving toward where the presenter would stand. Next, you would want to practice delivering brief remarks from that position before an empty room. Next, you would deliver a few remarks before the least threatening audience possible, in an environment that is as similar as possible. And so on.

Locations, size of audience, length of presentation, and the perceived "threat" level are called "variables." To be successful, each should be introduced in the sequence and intensity that the mind is most likely to accept.

This could consume more time than you care to spend—especially if you have to face an audience soon. Thus, I have developed a way to help people overcome this fear in as little as an hour—sometimes even less when the anxiety level isn't quite as high. We'll consider these in detail in the next few pages.

Thanks to the human ability to reason, the rational mind can generally help to accelerate the process, and apprehensive people can overcome negative mannerisms and feelings that manifest themselves when they have to face audiences.

Success can be yours when you realize that it is possible to control your thoughts and feelings. As you learn what you must do to achieve positive experience, you will become less concerned about what might happen in situations where you have lacked poise and confidence in the past. Then, when unpleasent experiences do occur, you will understand them better and know how to stay in charge.

When You Hit a Lapse

If you are like most people, perhaps one of your greatest fears as a presenter is that you will go blank right in the middle of your presentation. If you have ever stood before an audience and found yourself at a loss for words, you know the feeling. Even if you haven't, you might rank the situation high among your worst fears as a presenter.

You look from your notes or script to your audience, deliver a few words, and suddenly your mind goes blank. You look down at the printed words, and you can't find a thing to latch onto. As the stress builds, your mind seems to be floating away from your body.

Or you look down for help and find yourself, instead, staring at a sea of words. Panic sets in as you experience a feeling that must be akin to the last, futile breath of a drowning swimmer.

If you've been through this—or hope and pray that you never will be—here's a lifeline that may be able to help you.

First, let's consider why memory lapses occur: Usually, because the presenter has not slept well, has put in a long day, or has just arrived from a long trip without enough time to settle down before speaking. Lapses also occur when a distraction interrupts the speaker.

There are two types of distractions:

- *Audience* distractions can range from a group of people leaving the room to a server dropping a tray of dishes.
- *Personal* distractions might include dropping one's notes on the floor, accidentally disconnecting the microphone, or tripping on a riser.

Regardless of what caused the distraction, once you have lost your place, simply pause, and take a moment to recall the last words you said.

FILLING THE GAP

If you feel a need to fill the silence with words, you might try letting your body language acknowledge the lapse as you say something, such as this: "For those of you who may have already heard me speak before (or who received advance copies of my speech), please go on to my next point, and I'll catch up with you." However, if the stress keeps you from trying this light approach, you should move to the next step.

"SHIRT-TAILING"

Simply repeat the last part of the last sentence you delivered. Then add a further thought onto it. Next, repeat the last part of that sentence, and add to it. Keep going on in this manner as long as necessary.

Here is what will happen. The "shirt-tailing" technique of tagging on to the end of each thought will remove enough stress for your subconscious to calm down, and enable your conscious mind to remember where you were or to find a place in your notes or script where you can get back on track.

For example, let's say your last statement was: "This division must face the problems that have resulted from having doubled in size over the past ten months." Suddenly, you hit a memory lapse. Pause, then say, "It has doubled because we have added two new product lines."

Now, go on to say, "The two new product lines will enable us to provide choices to the customer that were not possible before, and this will enable us to attract new customers to our company." Then add: "Attracting new customers is something that is important to all of us in this era of intense competition."

You can continue this as long as you need to, but you should stop as soon as you can put yourself back on track. In many cases, you will find yourself "looping" or returning to your original thought. Don't let this come as a surprise.

The good news is that the loop closes precisely when the speaker has found his or her place again. There is a logic behind this: The speaker has total control over whether he or she keeps the loop open or closes it.

In the example we are using here, for instance, your next statement might be, "And facing competition by providing these two much needed product lines has caused the problems associated with the rapid growth of this division."

You have filled the gap with statements that make sense, and, with a little practice when you *don't* need it, shirt-tailing will enable you to come up with sensible sentences—unless you are in a dire panic, indeed.

Shirt-tailing also occupies your mind and frees it from such nervous thoughts as, "I've lost my place. What do I do now? What if I can't get my thoughts in order? I'm going to fail (lose my job, etc.)."

So, if you find yourself at a loss for words, pause to collect your composure. Then repeat each prior sentence, and add to it until you can return to your original thoughts—or find another place in your presentation where you can continue successfully.

It also helps to remember that audience members want you to succeed and (if they notice your dilemma at all) will be very supportive, especially when you need their patience and understanding.

Change Your Body, Change Your Emotions

Under stress, people tend to concentrate their tensions in one area more than others. You might feel it most across the forehead, in the temples, behind the eyes, in the throat, in the jaws, in the neck, in the shoulders, in the chest, in the stomach, in various joints, and so on. When stress occurs, some people become acutely concerned that the audience might detect the problem, so they overcompensate—often by tensing the area even more, as though to "stabilize" it. Regrettably, this usually intensifies the problem.

To counter this, you should locate the specific, physical areas where you feel stress the most. Then shake your hands loosely and rapidly, rag-doll fashion, clap them together, or swing them out to your sides and across your chest. This will stimulate circulation and warm your hands. Next, place your warmed hands on the stressful areas and concentrate on "bringing warmth" through your hands to relieve the stress.

The activity helps to burn off the stress by itself. It also takes your mind off your feelings. You can use this kind of displacement, or substitute, behavior in other ways to keep the body busy, to burn off the physical manifestations of stress, and to free your mind to focus on more beneficial behavior.

For example, you could deliver a simple paragraph or two and gesture excessively and broadly as you speak. You can also do this simple breathing exercise to help improve the oxygen flow to your brain: Inhale only through the nose for four counts. Hold the breath for four counts. Exhale for eight counts, pushing out all the remaining breath with the last count. Repeat the procedure twice.

Each time you feel your stress easing, tell yourself that you are feeling calmer. This will help reinforce your new stress-control skills and reassure your subconscious (where most learning takes place) that you are in control of the situation.

As the stress eases, so does the constricting tension that reduces the flow of blood throughout the body. Thus, oxygen is supplied more readily to the brain. This will also help put the mind at ease and reduce the risk of panic that might be caused by a perceived threat of oxygen starvation. It follows that when the mind no longer assumes that the whole being is threatened, it no longer needs to prepare for a fight/flight response. (Thus, you will avoid the added stress of having no "escape.")

Yawning and stretching exercises are also effective. Who has ever seen an uptight cat?

Law of Gravity

Many presenters feel that the pull of gravity impacts on the body and causes fatigue and stress. So they lie down, elevate their feet, and take the pressure off their spine, neck, and shoulders.

This position also helps circulate more oxygen through the blood stream and into the brain. This, in turn, helps encourage clearer thinking and lower stress levels.

Just before you face an audience you can burn off stress and pump up your adrenalin at the same time with some quick, physical activity. Do whatever it takes to get you going. Bounce on the balls of your feet. Do jumping jacks. Swing your arms out to the sides then bring them across your body in a slapping motion.

Thanks to the human ability to reason, you should be able to overcome your stress quickly when you can persuade your mind that you are, indeed, in charge.

Part of this has to do with the way you stand. As you release tension, you should assume increasingly confident postures. Don't lean on anything. Don't even shift your weight to one foot. Keep your body evenly balanced. Leaning creates pressure. Pressure causes muscle tension. Tension brings about stress, and the problems can worsen from there.

The old advice "chin up, stomach in, chest out, eyes straight ahead" still works. That's the stance of a confident person. To that you should also add: feet spread slightly apart, legs bent at the knees, shoulders relaxed, jaw tension released.

If you follow the guidance offered here, you will be able to deal emotionally with almost anything that happens during your presentation. Attitude is everything, and science has proven that these techniques can, indeed, help you through whatever situation might occur.

3
Body Language

Audiences form impressions of you before you say a word. Your total presentation consists of more than just content: It includes your voice and your body language. In fact, of the total message your audience receives, only 7 percent comes to them through content. The rest is comprised of your voice (38 percent) and your non-verbals (55 percent).

You are actually communicating from the moment you are introduced—sometimes even from the moment you walk into the room. Thus, your body language must convey the right message.

Emotional States and Their Corresponding Non-verbals

We all believe we know what certain non-verbals "mean." Most people would say that they can accurately predict a person's attitude from the body language (including face) that they display. In a sense, they may

---

IMPACT OF YOUR DELIVERY ON AN AUDIENCE

Albert T. Mehrabian

7 percent is content
38 percent is voice
55 percent is non-verbals

---

be right. However, I have found it to be a mistake to try to isolate any part of the body and attempt to draw meaning from whatever it is doing. This holds true even though there are several gestures whose interpretations have remained fairly consistent in our society over the years.

Gestures are still considered outward expressions of inner emotions. However, we now realize that the same gesture may have different meanings under different circumstances. For example, if someone rubs his or her eye—a gesture that is commonly thought to indicate suspicion—how would we know that this person simply wasn't itchy? Don't be too quick to say, "Do you doubt my word!?!"

Or, take yawning: People commonly interpret a yawn as a sign of boredom, but those who study the phenomenon say it may have other interpretations. A study of dogs' behavior, where the observations are easier to make than they are with humans because canine behavior is far less complex, indicates that when dogs yawn they may be processing a conflict between two behaviors. In fact, even yawning when one may desire to sleep instead of stay awake illustrates the point. It is a form of conflict resolution.

Here is yet another illustration of yawning as an expression of conflict between two behaviors—for an entirely different reason. I have found that dogs also yawn when they are being taught something new. As the learning (the transition between previous and new behavior) takes place, yawning occurs quite often.

So even yawning might not mean what we have stereotypically come to conclude that it means. When you see audience members yawn, don't assume they're bored. They may be learning what you have just talked about.

Science has come a long way since the Ray T. Birdwhistell studies of the 1950s, in which isolated gestures were studied for their presumed meanings. We have since learned that it is far more effective to consider individuals' non-verbals as a whole, in specific situations, and in context with whatever is occurring.

If you want to use body language to measure how your audience members are receiving you, consider the sum total of their signaling body parts, such as eyes, mouth, neck, shoulders, back, arms, legs, and their overall body postures, such as standing erect versus slumping.

Even flat, two-dimensional photographs can be "read" with considerable accuracy, and videotapes even more so. Thus, it should be even easier to read the non-verbals of participants in your audience. However, it takes learning to handle every other aspect of presentations delivery so well that you can pay attention to the signals.

Gestures and Postures

Some say the human body can transmit more than 20,000 separate and distinct gestures. This doesn't even consider the additional messages that can be transmitted by combining individual, non-verbal signals. For a presenter to try to observe even a fraction of that number, assign meaning to them, and then try to act on that information would be overwhelming. Thus, it makes even more sense to cluster and read non-verbal signals as a whole.

When examined this way, individuals' body language generally sorts into categories that you can readily identify even as you speak. Earlier, we considered the four-part personality theory overall and applied it to individual's words and non-verbals collectively. We will now expand on that discussion to enable you to look more closely at body language, alone, in terms of active and passive approach and avoidance signals.

Approach/Avoidance Signals

How do you know when audience members are with you, when they're not, and what their postures might tell you? Let's consider the many combinations that have somehow come to have meaning in people's lives.

Looking at their overall posture, here are some general cues:

- Relaxed and leaning forward with open posture—A possible Approach I.
- Relaxed and sitting upright with open posture—A possible Approach II.
- Tense and leaning to one side with closed posture—A possible Avoidance I.
- Tense and leaning back with closed posture—A possible Avoidance II.

Now check just their faces: Do they look angry or hostile? Do they look worried or defensive? Bored or dispassionate? Enthusiastic or eager? Active or involved? Supportive or understanding? Calm or complacent? Curious or puzzled?

How do you determine all this? It may not be easy at first to know how you sort and quantify all these signals, since you have been doing it intuitively—accurately or not—over a lifetime.

Perhaps you first notice the tilt of the person's head because it is the largest or most obvious cue. Is it tilted up? Down? Forward? Back? To the side? Held symmetrically and balanced?

Perhaps you next observe what the person's eyes are doing. Are the eyes looking toward you or away? If directly at you, does the intensity indicate a challenge or receptivity? Is the intensity missing, so that the person really doesn't seem to be looking at you at all? Is the person looking away? Up? Down? To the side? Is he or she looking at anything or anyone in particular or just gazing into thin air?

Perhaps you next notice the person's mouth. Is it relaxed? If so, is it open or closed? Is it tense? Are the lips up, down, straight across, or tilted to one side? Are they curved? Is the person smiling or frowning?

Now go on to consider the facial muscles in your "reading." Are they relaxed? How would you describe the look? Accepting? Bored? Are the facial muscles tense? Would you say they reflect support or antagonism? Is the brow furrowed or smooth?

It is amazing that this small cluster of signals can provide dozens and dozens of overall combinations and that even those can be fine tuned to provide hundreds more.

You can even develop comparable, although shorter, checklists for arms and hands and for legs and feet. You could also check to see how each of the groups is displayed in combination with the others.

For example, how would you interpret a person who was leaning back, staring down, smiling, with legs crossed at the knees and with arms folded and hands clenched? Try it out. See how it feels. Imagine someone else looking that way, or ask someone to assume that combination of signals for you. One interpretation is that the overall message will be one of skepticism, disbelief, cynicism, sarcasm, disagreement, strong opinion, and more. As you begin to observe others' non-verbals, you will be accomplished, indeed, if you can learn even to determine accurately who might be supporting or disagreeing with you, who might simply be attentive or inattentive, and who has you tuned in or out.

It would take a book dedicated to non-verbals alone to provide you with all the possible ways in which each of the signaling groups might be combined and how we might interpret each combination. A book on effective business presentations could not possibly go into that much detail. Most business presenters would not benefit proportionally from a discussion of body language in this depth.

Keep non-verbals in their proper perspective: Before you form any conclusions about what you see, consider whether the body language may have some root cause other than your presentation.

One sales executive told me this story in a seminar:

"I saw this man fidgeting and grimacing and I thought, 'Boy, this guy is having some real problems with what I'm saying.' I tried different ways to engage him and get him to change his posture, but I still got the same message. It was starting to get to me, but I didn't want to stop in the middle of my presentation and confront him with what I was observing, so I called a break.

"I walked over to him at once, and he immediately looked at me and asked: 'You don't happen to have a Rolaids do you?' So much for interpreting body language!"

The message? Regardless of what you think you see before you, check it out. It is often better to ask and find out what's behind the signals than to act inappropriately on false assumptions. After your presentation, when you take questions, non-verbals become even more evident and you will have an even better opportunity to discover what messages of any consequence lie behind any individual's body language.

Your Own Non-verbals

As a presenter, your audience is constantly observing your non-verbals, too. Just as you may try to read them, they may also be trying to read you. Your gestures and postures (along with your voice tones) do, indeed, send messages to your audience. So be sure they communicate the emotions you intend to convey.

There are no "right" or "wrong" gestures, postures, or facial expressions. They just need to be appropriate to the feeling you are trying to communicate, and in the proper intensity. I recall a videotaped television interview in which George Bush, who was at the time an ambassador, said he would be using "quiet diplomacy"—while he said this, he was shaking a doubled fist. A warning perhaps? A double meaning? A threat? An inconsistency or incongruity between words and gestures? Only Mr. Bush can say whether the gesture conveyed his underlying intentions.

Similarly, I once watched a labor negotiator on videotape say, "You can do anything you want," as he swept his hand out from his chest in a parallel motion toward and away from the listener. He continued, "I've got all the time in the world," as he punctuated each word with a series of karate chops. Did he convey his intentions? Perhaps so. Again, only he would know for certain.

By all means, then, use gestures. They are good for you. They lubricate your voice and relieve tension. They add visual interest and convey enthusiasm. They add punctuation to the messages you deliver. The point here is one of congruence: Be sure your motions reflect your emotions—or at least the ones you want to convey. Beyond that, it would be foolhardy to try to plan or force gestures.

A story circulates about a clergyman who sought a speech consultant's advice on gesturing—five minutes before a service. With no time for detailed counsel, the consultant said, "For now, just point up or point down." The minister took the advice. And this is how it came out at one of the most intense moments in his sermon: "And when that big roll call sounds up yonder," he said as he gestured upward with enthusiasm, "I'll be *there!*" And, before he could stop himself, he jabbed his finger toward the ground.

Force-fit gestures pose another, inherent, problem: They always come late. By the time the mind consciously thinks to gesture, picks one, and then tells the body to carry it out, the mouth has already spoken the words that the gesture should have accompanied. Mechanical gestures always occur about a beat too late. So decide ahead of time what emotions should accompany your words, get in touch with those emotions during your rehearsals, and then allow the gestures that reflect those emotions to occur naturally.

You may say, "I don't gesture." But, in fact, you do. It's just that you may not be in the habit of gesturing before audiences. Who knows, it may have something to do with the "old-country" advice that was frequently given to first-generation Americans who spoke English as a second language. Perhaps not wanting to be perceived as "foreigners," they believed that using one's hands might be regarded as a poor substitute for not knowing the right words in English.

When You Inhibit Gestures

One thing is certain: Nervous energy is bound to go somewhere. So, unless you gesture, you may find yourself clinging to the lectern as though it were the only thing in life that could keep you from drowning.

If you don't gesture, and if you don't cling, you're likely to do something else with your hands. Here are some things my workshop participants have observed in playbacks of their videotapes. I call the different types of substitute gestures: adjusting, stroking, picking, fiddling, scratching, and playing.

Adjusting—Microphones, note cards, hair (again, head or facial), glasses, and various items of clothing.

Stroking—Hair (head or facial), scarves, and neckties.

Picking—At lint, at food stains, at splinters on the wooden lectern, at knots in the mike cord, and even at blemishes.

Fiddling—With loose overhead frames, coffee cups, glasses, water pitchers, and their own handouts (and even those of other presenters).

Scratching—*Everything* that seemed to itch at the moment.

Playing—With microphone cords and stands, pencils, markers and chalk, string, rubber bands, paper clips, note cards, eyeglasses, chains, rings, other jewelry, clothing, loose change in pockets, and even their own fingers (cleaning one fingernail with another).

They also put their hands in and out of their pockets, and when they weren't doing any of these things, many kept their hands locked firmly together as though they had been fastened with bonding cement.

I frequently ask people before they see their video playback what they think they did with their hands while they were speaking. Most have no idea until they see the tape. Even then, some have said, "Noooo, I couldn't possibly have done *that*."

If you have any inhibitions about gesturing, set them aside—forever. Remember: Fifty-five percent of your total message comes through your body language, and 38 percent comes through your voice—which is aided by your gestures. If you want to get across the remaining 7 percent—the content portion of your impact on the audience—it is a good idea to pay close attention to this whopping 93 percent. There is no question: Natural gestures that spring from genuine emotions are an important part of any presentation.

The Lasting First Impression

Whenever you present information or respond to questions, your first few minutes can determine the lasting impression your audience will have of you. As a television commercial put it, "You never have a second chance to make a first impression." One way to think about that first impression is to consider this modified version of the Boy Scout Creed. I call it the Seven C's: A presenter is calm, courteous, caring, cheerful, competent, creative, and confident.

Calm presenters put audience members' minds at ease. They exude an air of being in charge, without appearing to be controlling. They use good eye contact and never interrupt others who are speaking. They do nothing that distracts as they listen attentively with their entire minds and bodies. Periodically, they provide feedback to show (or to ensure) that they are listening accurately.

Courteous presenters consider the needs of their audiences. They also listen attentively and give other speakers their total attention, or eliminate anything that may distract them or detract from their comments. They make special efforts to stay with other people's train of thought.

Caring presenters are especially sensitive to others' hopes, fears, dreams, disappointments, aspirations, and insecurities. They respect people's rights—or needs—to be as they are. They try to help others clarify their positions (but only *after* they have finished speaking).

Cheerful presenters can find the humor in any situation without letting it make them uptight. They pleasantly acknowledge the needs or desires of others and ask people what they feel is best for them or for the situations in which they find themselves. Then they reflect what they learn in the way they respond to that knowledge, constantly alert to opportunities to enhance others' self-esteem.

Competent presenters know their subject and have done their homework. They never seem self-effacing or overly apologetic in their dealings with others. Their ability to handle the task well helps to build confidence among those with whom they deal.

Creative presenters are adventuresome and find ways to capitalize on spontaneous opportunities for doing an even better job. They are especially alert to opportunities that audience members provide because they tune in to others' feelings and solicit feedback. Frequently, they ask such questions as, "What do you think? How do you feel about that?" They have developed a variety of ways to achieve rapport with people.

Confident presenters prepare as well as they can and recognize that doing their best is all that anyone can do. They exude warmth and encourage it in others. They are pleased by the achievements of others and let them know it.

Few people possess all these attributes—and certainly not all the time. However, try to watch those presenters who seem to come close to having them. Make your own checklist from this information and keep it handy when you attend their presentations. See how they "score," and note your reasoning. This will help you to benefit from role modeling, an important and highly effective technique for improving one's skills in any area.

With effort and experience you will learn to develop the best first— and lasting—impression that will enable you to build a positive relationship with any audience. When that occurs, you will have acquired a special attribute that can best be described by yet another "C"— *charisma*.

4
Your Voice

If audiences receive only 7 percent of your total message from the words themselves and 38 percent from your voice, you can see how important it is to cultivate a good speaking voice. You don't need to sound like a radio announcer, but you should care for and use your voice as though you were one.

When I first began speaking in public, I suffered from chronic colds and sinus problems and found that most "cold and sinus remedies"—especially nasal inhalants—actually made me feel worse when they wore off. Now, I rarely have a cold or any other illness, and I believe this has occurred for two reasons: 1. I take care of my voice like the important tool of my trade that it is. For example, I have learned to monitor the sound it puts forth, listening especially for the early signs of fatigue, stress, allergy, or a cold. 2. I have learned to have a new attitude toward stressful events, and I follow my own advice as outlined in this book.

Personal Hints

Here are some of the things I have found helpful for myself and for many of my clients: Avoid dampness, sudden changes in temperatures, drafts, and chills. Stay out of drying winds. Avoid smoke and fumes.

Don't strain your voice. Even coughing can cause more irritation than relief. Instead, try drinking water (not too chilled) more frequently. Note whether this reduces the amount of coughing you have experienced in the past.

If you are on the road, and the air in your hotel room is dry—as is often the case—consider filling your tub partially with water, or putting water in the ice bucket that most hotels provide and placing it on a towel near your bed.

If you find yourself coming down with a cold, breathe through a towel, handkerchief, piece of gauze, or any other kind of material—even your scarf or the turned-up collar on your jacket or coat. If you are desperate, you can even keep your hand in front of your mouth and nose as you breathe. Research has shown that doing any of these will raise the temperature around this area high enough to kill the cold germs and shorten the life of the common cold.

INSTANT MOISTURE

If your throat suddenly goes dry, you can produce moisture temporarily by nipping the tip of your tongue between your teeth. Try it right now. It works. Just don't substitute doing this for a visit to your doctor if you suffer from chronic dry throat.

To make this instant-saliva technique more effective in the future, try it again now. However, this time, think of sucking on a lemon as you close your teeth on your tongue. Over the next day or so, repeat the process whenever you happen to think of it.

Rather quickly, you will be able to produce some valuable moisture reliably either by thinking of a lemon *or* by biting your tongue. As we saw in Chapter One, you have created a conditioned response to two different stimuli—one physical, the other emotional.

VITAMIN C

We will discuss diet later, but I think vitamin C is worth considering here. Many current studies show the importance of maintaining an adequate level of this vitamin to ward off or reduce the intensity of short-term colds and related infections. Doing so may help keep your voice in top working order.

Some of those researchers who advocate vitamin C supplements advise that it must remain in the system in sufficient quantities at all times to serve any useful purpose: It apparently does little good if taken only when one already has a cold or other respiratory infection and could leave the system vulnerable if discontinued too rapidly afterward.

I believe in supplementing my own diet with vitamin C (and other nutrients) because my eating regimen often lacks consistency due to my professional schedule, and I don't seem to obtain the vitamins I need in sufficient quantities. However, everyone's body is different, and whether to take vitamin C supplements is a matter of personal choice—one on which you might want to seek the guidance of a *knowledgeble* professional. (Many doctors will concede that they receive minimal training in nutrition and do not feel qualified to comment about it.)

BREATHING AND CONTROL

Learn to support, through proper breath control, every sound that comes from your diaphragm (the partition of muscles and tendons between your chest and abdominal cavities). Two books that I have found personally helpful and still refer to periodically are: *The New Voice— How to Sing and Speak Properly* by Alan Greene and *Voice Power* by Evelyn Burge Bowling. Between the two, you will learn far more about the specifics of cultivating a good speaking voice than a book on business presentations can possibly provide.

Honing Your Vocal Tools

Your voice can perform many functions to help you get your message across. Some of its powers include range, volume, pace, rate, intensity, inflection, and even pauses. You should also consider how you articulate or pronounce your words.

RANGE

Speak within a *range* that is normal for you. Don't try to position your voice to an uncomfortable level. More people create vocal strain by trying to pitch their voices lower than higher because they think that a lower voice sounds more authoritative. However, if the outcome is strain and raspiness, your voice will sound even less commanding.

VOLUME

Volume should be comfortable and appropriate to the circumstances under which you are speaking. I have heard an executive go from total dependency on microphones—even for audiences of only 50 people—to the ability to address 500 people without any amplification other than what her own vocal instrument provides. She now speaks in an ample, articulate voice that projects authority—while still sounding considerate.

PACE

Pace is also important. Your speech sounds rapid to most people when you are clipping along at about 200 words per minute. By contrast, it sounds slow to most listeners when you get below 100 words per minute. Why does pace vary? It may be a regional phenomenon, a response to stress (or a reflection of its absence), or the result of the speaker's being either a visual person (rapid) or a tactile or kinesthetic one (slow).

In any case, the key to success in most situations is to start at about 120 words per minute, and then level off at between 125 and 150. You should record yourself on tape to check your own natural pace. For variety and dramatic impact, from time to time you can speak more rapidly, more slowly, or even in a staccato fashion in which you emphasize *each individual word.*

INTENSITY

This reflects the tension in your voice and how you emphasize words. Consider how someone might react if you touched an item on which she had just told you the paint was still wet. She might smile sympathetically and say, "I *told* you not to touch that." Or, she might clench her teeth, lower her voice, and enunciate every word as she says (as if to a disobedient child): "I . told . you . not . to . touch . that." Although you are only reading these words on paper, I'm sure you *heard* the difference.

INFLECTION

Inflection or emphasis is also an important tool for speakers. So much so that I have developed a series of speech "mark-up" symbols that you can use to annotate your speech text much as a musician might score a piece of music.

Marking a Script for Voice Dynamics

Here are the symbols I have clients use to mark the rehearsal copy of their speech. It should be double-spaced and set up for delivery according to the Eye-Cue™ method discussed in Chapter 11.

<	**Louder or Faster**	⎱ mark above the words
>	**Softer or Slower**	⎰
⁓	**Emphasize**—mark beneath the words	
//	**Long Pause**	⎱ mark between the words
/	**Short Pause**	⎰
⌒	**Tie Together**	⎱
↑	**Voice Up**	⎰ mark above the words
↓	**Voice Down**	⎰

Until you begin to work on your speech, consider what you might do with even one sentence just by emphasizing a different word each time you read it aloud:

Mary is always ready to blame someone.
(More so than Bob, John, or Tonia is.)
Mary *is* always ready to blame someone.
(There's no question about it.)
Mary is *always* ready to blame someone.
(It never fails.)
Mary is always *ready* to blame someone.
(But she may not follow through.)
Mary is always ready to *blame* someone.
(But she's stingy about giving credit.)
Mary is always ready to blame *someone.*
(Anyone at all.)

Try the same sentence again, but this time vary the dynamics, using the symbols differently each time. For additional practice, see what you might do with this one:

"Will somebody please tell me where we're going." (Hint: You can create several more meanings by emphasizing more than one word each time you read the sentence out loud.)

PAUSES

A pause enables your audience to catch up with you, to process your observations, and to prepare for or anticipate what is coming. Pauses are like the rests in a piece of music. Some are quite short, others fairly long. However, each serves the same purpose—making the piece more effective for the listener. Pauses in a speech do the same when they come at appropriate times.

ARTICULATION

How *articulate* are you? Here we are not talking about dialect, but rather about the proper pronunciation—and even enunciation—of words. One of my favorite examples of the confusion poor enunciation can cause occurred when a local music group sang "Seventy-six Trombones." I kept hearing words that I thought were "horse spitoons." To my amusement, I later learned that the actual words were "horse *platoons.*"

If you are concerned about how particular words should be pronounced, or how to pronounce words in general, listen to national newscasters on radio and television. They speak standard English, and their diction is fairly reliable. You might also practice using the pronunciation guide found at the bottom of the pages of most dictionaries, which is often explained in more detail in the front of them.

Lists of commonly mispronounced words—and their correct pronunciations—abound. If you have serious concerns, ask your local librarian or a member of the speech or English department at your community college if they will help. You might even consider consulting a speech pathologist if you feel that would be appropriate.

IF YOU STUTTER

Several years ago, I saw a seminar leader display an ability to help people who stuttered and whose problems made it difficult for them to face audiences. I have modified this person's technique, and have used it over the years with some success. (With the passage of time, I can no longer recall the name of the speaker, and regret not being able to give him or her proper credit.)

If you feel you have a special difficulty speaking smoothly, it might help to consider that everyone stutters or stammers at times. When President Kennedy was under pressure to name a new postmaster general, he was asked about this in a news conference. His ability to keep a sense of humor and think on his feet even under pressure was evident when he replied that he was considering many types of people— including even those with "a postal background." The reporters loved it, and so has everyone who has seen this verbal exchange on videotape. Not one person then, or in all the years since, has ever commented on JFK's having said, ". . . even a, uh, . . . uh, . . . uh, . . . even a postal background." His poise and self-acceptance carried him through.

I have used the following technique with my clients who have had what they considered to be serious problems with stuttering when they had to face audiences. If this is a personal concern, you might try it too.

Monitor your self-talk closely whenever you are having a conversation. If you catch yourself thinking about stuttering when you are about to speak or while you are speaking, jab your thumbnails into your index fingers. Pause and think about how you would like to finish your sentence. Then extend both index fingers toward each other and allow them to touch, as though they were "completing the circuit" *for* you. As they do, you will find yourself able to complete your thought smoothly even as you focus on the next one. While the technique does not work for all people, it's certainly worth trying several times to see whether it can help you. Give it a chance.

STATIC

Finally, when evaluating how you use your voice, you need to consider *"static."* This term includes all words and sounds that do not contribute to good speech. We are talking about such words as, "it's like," "you know," and "okay." Listen also for such "filler" sounds as, "uh" or "and," and even "and, uh." They contribute nothing to effective speech, although we all find ourselves using them, or others, from time to time—frequently when we are tired, ill-prepared, or under stress.

To get rid of these empty words, first become aware of your habit of using them. Prepare yourself properly to reduce stress, and keep your mind focused ahead—on your next thought. When you feel a static word coming on, don't say anything, and then force yourself to say the next "real" word that will contribute to your meaning.

Using Your Voice to Motivate

I was once told a purportedly true story about a political speech that says absolutely nothing, but which, through the use of delivery techniques alone—primarily voice dynamics—has caused politicians to be elected. Although I have never heard the speech, the story sounds plausible. After all, I have heard more than a few campaign speeches that came awfully close to doing just that.

When your voice conveys appropriate emotions, you will generally gain the empathy of your audience. However, you may want to be aware of some negative voice characteristics and of how they are perceived.

Martin G. Groder, writing in "Boardroom Reports," offered some interesting observations on how people use their voices. He said that a *flat tone* often expresses a subordinate's disagreement with those in authority and is usually preceded by a voice with a high-energy level and lots of animation. *Whining* voices generally indicate a helpless, hopeless, or frightened person, perhaps one who harbors secret fears. A *loud* voice can indicate a person who demands to be heard, but may not have confidence in his own authority. A *mumbler* may be trying to "hide" her words, work things out audibly, or fill possible silence with sound. A *prodding* tone often reveals a person who wants to put the listener on the defensive, and may indicate aggression. It is frequently used by someone who feels threatened. If your voice falls into any of these categories, you can practice modifying your tone, inflection, volume, and articulation to have your voice reflect the kind of emotions you might find more useful and constructive.

When you speak, keep in mind the many tools that you have for getting your convictions across to your audience. Keep these tools finely honed, and know which to use and how to use them. Then use them wisely and well. Both you and your audiences will benefit.

Other Considerations

To use your voice best, try to ease the tension in your throat, jaw, and facial muscles. This is where you produce sound. If the problem is mild, you can often ease the tension with proper rest and by speaking in a more comfortable range. However, if you have considerable tension, chronic raspiness, or other recurring problems when you speak, your voice may indicate that there is stress elsewhere in your life, and you may need medical attention.

For problems such as snapping or popping in your jaw area, consult your dentist. For other difficulties, you may want to consult a professional speech or voice coach or a speech therapist.

Protecting your voice and using it correctly is one of the most important steps you can take if you want to be an effective presenter and have a long career facing audiences.

5
Clothes, Food, and Rest

When you face an audience, your clothes become very important. Nearly every job in every organization has a dress code. Often it is unspoken and cloaked behind a veil of what seems to be permissiveness. Don't believe what others may be paying lip service to: Instead, notice what people in jobs comparable to, or higher than, yours actually wear. Here are some tips to help you dress appropriately.

COLOR
When in doubt, brown is out. Too many surveys have indicated that brown conveys an image of humility, of lower status, and, sometimes, of servitude. In more than 25 years of working with highly placed executives, I have rarely seen a chief executive in a brown suit. One exception was the executive director of a nonprofit organization. Another was a lobbyist who deliberately dressed in brown as part of his "low-threat" image. For *any* presentation, gray or blue is appropriate. Wear the lighter shades in warm weather, the darker in cold weather. For managers, a muted pinstripe is always acceptable.

Accessories should generally be pale blue or gray, with burgundy ties, scarves, or shawls (if tastefully done). Men should wear black shoes. Women can wear black shoes, or they can coordinate with blue, gray, or burgundy—again, lighter shades in warm weather.

ATTIRE
Women have several options provided they remain within the "code." They can wear suits, dresses, coordinates, skirts and blazers or, if tastefully put together, skirts and blouses. Men need to wear suits,

although dressy blazers are acceptable in some situations. Vests—while attractive—tend to add weight to both men and women when they are seated (and even on television when standing).

Shoes should be conservative and reflect good taste: Men should pay particular attention to whether their peers and superiors generally wear dress slip-ons, lace-ups, or wing tips. The heels and soles of the shoes must not appear worn, and shoes must be well-polished. Women should avoid open-toe shoes and higher heels because they are impractical (especially in rain, snow, or cold weather).

Men's socks must be high enough to keep bare legs from being exposed when they sit with their legs crossed. Women should carry extra stockings to avoid appearing in public with a run.

Keep jewelry to a minimum and wear nothing that dangles, flashes, or otherwise distracts or calls attention to itself. Carry nothing in your pockets. Bulges are not attractive, and people under stress tend to fidget with items in their pockets.

Additional Tips

If you have done everything possible to determine the proper attire, and you still aren't sure what to wear, dress conservatively and follow these additional guidelines:

- Your accessories, such as briefcase, pen, etc., must be of top quality. Never carry plastic pens or pocket liners for pens.
- Have all buttons in place and tightly secured.
- Adjust your tie or scarf *before* you face an audience or interview.
- Your nails must be neatly manicured.
- Try to schedule your appearance in the morning before new beard overshadows your appearance or before your makeup begins to fade. If you must face an important audience after midday, men should shave again, and women should reapply makeup.
- Check to see that your hair is neatly combed or brushed. Scissors or hairspray can take care of that wisp of fly-away hair that won't stay down at the last minute. Women can have their hair done, but should not experiment with a new hairdo. Men should *not* get a new haircut within three days of a presentation. Close haircuts tend to convey the impression that a man cuts pennies by having his hair

cut short to prolong the time between haircuts. On television, new haircuts can make you look scalped. At the other extreme, men should never appear to need a haircut.

- Women's skirts should range from mid-knee to about an inch below, regardless of what's in "style." This is especially true on stage where the audience is below the presenter, or on television where camera angles are sometimes low. Men's trousers should be long enough to break slightly at the crease.
- If you have to do any of your own physical setup before the presentation, remove your jacket. Some people even slip an old shirt over their dress, blouse, or shirt while they are setting up. This helps avoid disasterous spills or tears in the clothing you will wear for your presentation.
- If you have been traveling, change to a fresh shirt or blouse before you do your presentation. If your suit appears wrinkled or rumpled, either change it or touch it up with a portable steamer.

By reassuring yourself that you look good before you face an audience, you will have overcome a lot of the stress commonly associated with presentations and interviews.

How and What to Eat

Eat a protein breakfast. Take a multivitamin. Take a B-complex vitamin. Do whatever you can to help your body get the nourishment it needs to put forth its best effort. You can't run a jet aircraft on diesel fuel. Only the purest, highest-quality products should go into your "engine"— especially before you speak.

Avoid heavy, starchy, or carbohydrate-laden foods. They will make you feel tired. Avoid any foods with excessive roughage. Natural cereals, whole-grain muffins, nuts, and berries can stick in the throat and pose problems when you speak.

Also, avoid extremely hot or cold beverages just before you face an audience. Cold constricts the muscles; heat expands them. Both pose problems for speakers. You should also avoid milk and cheese products *just* before you speak. They tend to thicken mucus in the throat. Many speakers find it helpful to sip a moderately warm cup of tea with honey and lemon, or a slightly flat cola that is approximately room temperature. Make certain that you sip slowly.

Throat Conditions

If you need to reduce the symptoms of a cold, allergy, hayfever, or sinus condition, avoid antihistamines unless they are absolutely essential. Instead, take something that will help keep your throat moist. As a last resort, you might try a product, such as Glyoxide(r), that has a glycerine base and is used in dental hygiene. Place a few drops on the back of your tongue before you speak and allow the liquid to ease down your throat and coat it. This will also help overcome the initial dry-throat syndrome that speakers often experience before they address an audience.

Avoid alcohol-based products. This is not the time for a brandy "cure" for your cold. Simply put, alcohol and other drugs won't help you speak better or become a better speaker.

Get the Right Kind of Rest

You will benefit from a good night's sleep before a presentation, or even a brief rest about an hour before speaking. It will give your mind a chance to recycle, to clear itself of any excesses that it might be harboring. It also enables you to concentrate and to focus clearly on your message.

Travel without Stress

When you log over 100,000 miles a year on the road as I have done, you learn a number of "tricks" about eating, attire, rest, tickets, hotels, transportation, and everything else that might be stressful. Even if you don't plan to make more than one trip this year, you can benefit from these tips.

Order your travel tickets well before your trip and ask a lot of questions—especially about scheduling. Sometimes you can avoid changing planes or having your luggage make a separate trip just by changing your flight by a few minutes.

If you do have to make connecting flights, know where they depart. Anyone who has used Chicago's O'Hare International Airport, for example, makes certain they won't have to run to reach a connecting airline or flight before the plane departs. Allow yourself a half hour of ground time, or longer, between connecting flights.

After you order your tickets, either pick them up yourself or have them hand-delivered. Don't assume that the tickets are correct—check them against your itinerary. Mistakes happen. Many years ago, I was headed for Dallas–Fort Worth via Atlanta International. When I arrived in Atlanta for the connecting flight, I learned that my ticket for that leg of the trip was written for a departure at almost exactly the right time on the right airline, but for a plane to Miami. Mercifully, a helpful ticket agent got me on the correct plane.

When you order your tickets, ask if a meal will be served. If so, request a special meal. Most airlines offer low-fat, low-cholesterol, low-salt, kosher, vegetarian, and other options. These meals must be prepared individually and are consequently better in my opinion than the prepackaged fare the rest of the passengers receive. You might also want to bring a protein snack of your own, such as peanuts or cheese. If you have problems with air pressure, you might want to bring chewing gum. Once in the air, drink water. Plane cabins notoriously lack humidity, and your throat will benefit from the extra moisture.

Also, when you order your tickets, request an aisle seat unless you intend to sleep through the entire flight. Aisle seats give you more shoulder and leg room and more freedom to stretch your legs. Try to avoid what are called the "bulkhead" seats—the ones that have the cabins' divider wall in front of you. They provide no room for underseat storage, and most airlines put passengers with babies in those seats.

When you pack, first write out your list, then strip it down to the minimum. Set as your goal the ability to carry everything you need directly onto the plane. Even if the airline has a good record for luggage handling, carryons save you from having to walk to a distant luggage area and wait to retrieve your belongings before you can get underway.

Generally, for a trip that requires two to five overnights, I pack two suits, two neckties, and a fresh shirt, underwear, and socks for each day. Women can generally follow the same rule, substituting as appropriate.

Wear three-season clothing year-round. You will rarely be outdoors long enough to need heavy wool. Top-quality wool blends will wrinkle least.

A trench coat with a zip-out lining, a wool scarf, and a pair of gloves are all the outerwear I've ever needed, except in extremely cold and windy cities in the winter. Then, I carry a full-length, down-filled coat that compresses into a small bundle and earmuffs that tuck into a pocket.

Don't pack your regular-sized containers of shampoo, hairspray, and so on. They take up too much room and add too much weight. Put just what you need into small plastic containers that have a reliable seal. Put these into a sealable plastic bag, for good measure, and then put that into a leak-proof kit for personal items. Using the same logic, take small containers for other items, such as shaving cream, toothpaste, deodorant, and the like.

Follow these instructions and you should be able to travel with one carry-on bag and another that tucks under your seat. Avoid a briefcase unless you feel that it is essential. My carryon has a side pouch for easy access on the flight. In it, I carry a copy of my presentation, my client file, a spare pen (they tend to stop writing in the air), and whatever book I am reading.

Unless I will be on the road for at least three days, I concede that I will never get to the hotel's sauna or pool, so I don't bother to bring a swimsuit or a robe. (I have given up trying to find the energy to use an exercise room, so I don't need to pack sweats and athletic shoes.) On longer trips, I carry a set of casual clothes for brief ventures to whatever attractions the city may offer.

When you check into your hotel, leave a wake-up call. When you arrive at your room, call down for messages—don't ask for them at the front desk. Calling is more certain to alert the operator that you have registered and are in that room. Leave another wake-up call, and set your alarm to go off five minutes later.

SLEEPING

If you have difficulty falling asleep, drink a glass of warm milk. Warming it releases chemicals that are known to help the brain relax. You can also do light stretching exercises and take a hot shower just before going to bed. As in all other stressful situations, make sure your self-talk is positive. Don't tell yourself, "I can't sleep." Instead, say: "I have done my best. I have prepared myself for tomorrow. Now I'm feeling very relaxed, my eyes are growing heavy. I can feel my head, arms, legs, my whole body slowly easing, relaxing deeper and deeper into the bed as I let go and enjoy a comfortable, restful sleep." As you say this, try to have your words match your breathing rate, slowing down more and more with each affirmation.

If you need more help, relax each part of your body progressively. Start with your toes. Tense them. Then allow them to relax as you tell yourself that your toes are now relaxed. Work your way up your body in this manner until you reach your stomach. Then shift out to your fingers and work your way back in until you reach your stomach again.

This time, however, focus on the muscles in your buttocks, then the small of your back, gradually working up your spine. When you reach your shoulders, switch to the top of your head, and work down through all your facial muscles (eyes, ears, nose, mouth, and jaw). Move to your neck, and follow the same procedure.

Finally, if you are still awake, try to tense every muscle in your body all at once. Then let go. As you release, make a mental picture of anything that you find tranquil and peaceful. Hold that image and tell yourself that you are sinking warmly, deeply, and pleasantly into total relaxation.

Don't try this now, however. We have more work to do.

JET LAG

Talking about sleep raises the question of jet lag. I have no solution because sometimes I feel "up" after a trip, sometimes I feel exhausted, and sometimes I feel no effects at all. My best recommendation is to listen to what your mind and body are trying to tell you, and do whatever you feel will help you best.

Research by scientists at Harvard University, Massachusetts General Hospital, and Tufts University has demonstrated that severe cases of jet lag can be treated with a hormone called melatonin, which is produced in the brain's pineal gland and has no known side effects. So if you have serious concerns about jet lag, ask your physician about this.

6
Preparing to Speak

If you're like many who find themselves facing audiences, you already know about criticism. In fact, you may have already had your fill of it over a lifetime. If so, that may account, in part, for any vocal or physical stress that you may have felt even at the thought of speaking before a group. Under these circumstances, you may choose not to have someone critique your rehearsals.

However, whether or not you have someone help you improve your performance (notice we did not say, "tell you what you're doing wrong"), you might consider this approach. Rehearse with both audio-cassette and videocassette recorders. They spare you from having to try to make a mental note of something you just did or said—even as you are speaking—in the hopes of being able to do something about it later.

There's no special magic to this: Use either one for "drafting" and note taking, although the audio recorder will be less distracting for this first rehearsal. You should also use the audio recorder to practice vocal technique and the video recorder to practice non-verbals.

Rehearse for Retention

Deal with drafts and note taking first. Record only your ending. Play it back and polish any words, phrases, and sequences of thought that you feel can be improved. Do the same with your middle. Finally, do this with your beginning. Although it may not make much sense to you at this point to do this in reverse order, you will soon learn more about the value of having your destination made clear and firm in your mind before you work on any other part of your speech.

48

As you rehearse, pay attention only to the structure of your talk, how readily you can speak the words, and how logically your thoughts flow. Listen from the audience's perspective for places where you can improve your content with "sparklers," such as those you will discover in Chapter Nine.

Look through the revised speech and mark a copy for voice dynamics, the way you believe you will want to deliver the words. Do this in pencil. You may want to change it once you hear it.

Make a second recording with all the dynamics in place. Play it back one more time and fine tune your script. You can use a pen for your markup symbols now.

Next, set up your video recorder, start it running, and walk to your lectern. If you don't have one where you are rehearsing, place a cardboard box on a table or do something equally creative.

In your first videotaping, you will only practice your walk off. Correct off. How you leave when you're finished has a profound impact on your audience—almost as much as how you walk on and begin. First and last impressions are significant, indeed.

With your recorder running, and the lens on the widest angle possible to take in every move you make—even away from the lectern— position yourself at the lectern and make your final point. Now, do what you have to do to leave.

Play the tape back, starting at where you began to speak your final words. Did you maintain eye contact during those last, all-important sentences? Good. Or were you looking down? For shame. Did you pick up your notes to take them with you? Good. Did you bang them together like a deck of cards? For shame. Did you remove your microphone if you were using a clip-on or a cord-type? Good. Did you "garrote" yourself? For shame. Did you look at the audience as you returned to your seat? Good. Did you heave a sigh of relief? For shame.

Now, tape your entire ending. That's correct, tape the ending. You'll find out why in Chapter Nine.

Put all the dynamics—voice and body language—into your ending. Don't concern yourself with content during this rehearsal. It really is difficult to do two things at once—at the start of any new learning experience. You're already taping, performing, and working on your non-verbals. That's enough for now. Your content will return later as you polish these skills.

In this rehearsal you will probably find yourself wondering what happened to all the gestures you thought you were using. Here's some insider's knowledge: People rarely find that they have overdone gestures when they see the playback. Oh yes: Did you find that you totally forgot your walk off? This is not uncommon at this stage of rehearsal. Work on it off camera right now if you did forget.

Next, go back and tape your middle, and play that back. Finally, do the same with your beginning. (Pssst: Remember your walk up before you deliver your opening.)

Now, take a break, and don't even look at your notes. Then go back and deliver the entire talk in its logical order: Walk up, beginning, middle, ending, and walk off.

If all this sounds "unnatural," remember that learned behavior is not "natural." Learning is a process that comes with time and should continue as long as we live. To quote an old adage, "The good get better."

If you have asked someone to help you with your critique, or if you want to do your own more formally, the evaluation checklist that follows will help.

Improving Your Gestures

If you have found through your rehearsal that you need to practice putting more oomph into your voice and body, try this exercise. It has helped innumerable speakers over the past decade.

Read the following aloud. Exaggerate your voice dynamics. Gesture as broadly as you can. Go to extremes with your hand, arm, and body movements. Think of yourself as the athlete who pole vaults 17 feet in practice to win the meet at just 15 feet.

GESTURE EXERCISE
The new sales person rushed into the room
Threw his briefcase on the table
Spun into a tight circle and
Raced back out the door.
Suddenly, he threw the door open again.
Loaded down with AV equipment,
He grumbled as he staggered to
The front of the conference room
Dropped everything on a nearby table
And wiped the sweat from his brow—
Vowing to never be late again.

Just for fun, and for an eye-opening outcome, videotape yourself doing this exercise. Again, overdo it. However, when you watch the replay, don't be surprised to find that your performance doesn't look as extreme as it may have felt while you were doing it.

SPEAKER APPRAISAL

Here is a list of the major elements I use to help my clients critique their presentations. To critique your own rehearsal, put an asterisk alongside each point you feel you handled well. Put an "X" alongside each point you feel you need to work on further. Under "Comments," note what you like or what you feel needs improvement. Note: You do not have to put a mark beside each category.

DATE: _____

Comments

"Walk up" or Approach   _____ _____

Gestures   _____ _____
Facial Expression   _____ _____
Eye Contact   _____ _____
Poise   _____ _____
Movement   _____ _____

Voice Level   _____ _____
Pacing   _____ _____
Modulation   _____ _____
Enunciation   _____ _____
Convictions   _____ _____

Ending   _____ _____
Middle   _____ _____
Beginning   _____ _____
"Sparklers"   _____ _____

Use of AV   _____ _____
Use of Mike   _____ _____
Use of Lectern   _____ _____
Use of Other Equipment   _____ _____

Handling of Questions   _____ _____
Handling of Questioners   _____ _____
Scoring of Positive Points   _____ _____

There is an important lesson here: You have a lot more latitude for both voice and body dynamics in speech delivery than you may have thought.

Another insider observation: I can assure you that when you actually face an audience, you will tend to diminish both gestures and voice dynamics anyhow. So, overrehearse these now, and your actual presentation will be far more effective.

Loosening Up

As with any exercises, you should consult with your physician or other health-care professional before undertaking a program of physical activity. Once you have done so, you will find that the exercises here will help you prepare to deliver a speech.

If you have special physical considerations, please keep them in mind when you consider the exercises described here. And if you have found other exercises especially helpful, keep using them—perhaps integrating them with those that follow.

As we have already seen, when you free your body of tension, your mind will become calmer. Many of my clients who experience the stress of TMJ (temporo-mandibular-joint syndrome) can get enough momentary relief to make their presentations when they use the exercise that follows (in conjunction with the other exercises—especially the "warm-hands" exercise—discussed in Chapter Two. They simply raise their heads off their shoulders, using only their own neck muscles to do so. As they do, they imagine that someone is cradling their heads gently and is lifting them lightly toward the ceiling. Many report that this seems to take the stress off their jaw muscles, and they also feel less stressful generally.

Other Stress Relievers

Recognize your stress and anxiety, and then take physical action to reduce it. First, raise your shoulders toward your ears. Imagine that someone has just hung you up in a closet with a coat hanger, and your feet are barely touching the ground. As you lift your shoulders, feel the light, comfortable stretching that occurs. Hold for two counts, and then let your shoulders drop like a wet washcloth. Do this ten times. If you want to yawn at any time during these exercises, do so.

Next, stretch your neck out, gently and slowly, and start curving your back over, so that you face the floor. Picture a giraffe easing down as you do this. Allow your head to lower slowly toward the floor. Do this ten times.

Now, do it one more time, but when your head is as far as you can extend it comfortably, look up slowly toward your left ear. Allow gravity to bring it back to the center. Then look up slowly toward your right ear. Allow it to drop to the center again, and return to your upright position. Do this ten times.

Next, extend your elbows out to your sides, and hold your hands toward your stomach. Using only your shoulders, trace circles in the air with your elbows. Do this forward ten times. Lower your arms for four counts. Then resume the elbows out position again. Now trace the circles to the rear ten times. Lower your arms.

Now face the palms of your hands in toward your sides and bring your arms behind you as you have seen racing swimmers do before they dive into the pool. Your thumbs are pointing down. Gradually rotate them up as high as you can. Hold for two counts. Then rotate them as far as you comfortably can in the opposite direction. Hold for two counts. Then allow your arms to return to your sides. Do this ten times.

Next, spread your feet to a comfortably wide stance, like two legs on a sturdy tripod. Shift most of your weight to your right side, and bend over from the waist until you can feel a gentle tug running down behind your *left* leg. Raise your upper body up and down enough to experience this tug ten times. Return to an upright position for four counts. Now repeat the procedure to the opposite side.

Reach both hands high over your head, and imagine yourself plucking two large grapefruit out of a tree. Stretch your fingers widely as though to grasp the fruit before you bring your hands back down to your sides. Do this four times.

On the fourth reach, slowly bring your arms back down. As you do, imagine that the grapefruit have grown suddenly heavy, and that you have to resist having the weight pull your arms down too rapidly.

Up to now, you have been exercising to reduce tension. Unless we go further, you may be ready for a nap instead of a speech. So, follow along.

Spread your feet comfortably apart, and extend your arms to your sides. Look at your left hand, and gently (!) allow your eyes and hand to move toward your left rear. Return to center, and do the same thing to your right. If you are comfortable with this exercise, and are not putting any uncomfortable stress on your lower back, you can speed up the motion—reaching only as far as you can do so comfortably. Do this ten times.

Rise up on the balls of your feet, balancing on your toes as much as possible and as well as you can. Allow your shoulders to go limp. Begin a bouncing motion without allowing your heels to touch the ground and while keeping your toes in contact with the ground at all times. Do this ten times.

Repeat the above exercise, but this time add one more thing: Stretch your mouth open slowly, feeling the comfortable tension of the muscles inside. Picture a kitten putting everything it has into the biggest yawn possible. (Did you just yawn or think about yawning, when you read this? If so, you will learn these stress reducers very quickly. If not, yawn anyway. It gets rid of stress.)

Skilled athletes never enter a competition without loosening up and aligning their mental processes toward the event. Skilled speakers know that facing audiences requires them to take a similar approach.

Do these exercises about five minutes before you go on. In fact, do them just before each rehearsal. The repeated association between warm-up exercises and doing well in rehearsal will carry over to each speaking engagement and make the exercises even more effective before you face audiences.

Part Two
Taking Charge of Your *Subject*

7
Targeting Your Message

Just as it is important for you to take charge of your *self,* you also must take charge of your *subject.* In this part of the book, you will explore new ways to address the factors that motivate audiences, build support, and enhance recall. You will learn my copyrighted technique for assembling a speech that will enable you to forget any concerns you may have had about "outlining." You will learn about humor, a note-card system that makes absolute sense, a new way to make a script more readable, and more.

Content may account for only seven percent of the audience's total impression, but that is precisely why it becomes such a high priority at this stage. In addition, many of the techniques discussed here will enable you to feel even more at ease before audiences.

What You Should Know about Audiences

When you face an audience, always remember that most audience members are supportive. Most people attend your presentations because you have information that can benefit them. They want you to succeed in sharing your ideas because that is in their own best interest.

Audiences are very forgiving. They assume that you must know something that they don't—even if they are authorities on the subject. A speaker who once addressed a group of management-level psychologists and psychiatrists suddenly found himself describing and using a technique that came directly from the behavioral sciences.

When he realized this, he became self-conscious and a little apprehensive. He finished that point and quickly returned to his main topic. When the talk was over, no fewer than three people out of an audience of about 60 Ph.D.s told him that they had not considered the point he had made in the context in which he presented it. They thanked him for sharing it. Had they noticed his apprehension? Not a bit. They had been too busy taking in what he had to say.

I'm told that a young cello soloist once thought his arm would drop off his body during a concert when he looked up to see the great maestro, Pablo Casals, seated in one of the front rows. Backstage later, Casals visited briefly with the young man. "Oh, maestro," he pleaded, "I feel so humiliated. How could I have even presumed to play before *you?*" "Nonsense," Casals responded. He asked permission to pick up the young man's cello, and said, "You know the passage that you bowed like this? Well, I have had troubles with that forever! Tonight, I learned from you."

And that—the opportunity to learn something new—is the reward that most audience members seek.

Developing an Audience Profile

To achieve your goals, you must know as much about your audience as possible. This will help ensure that your message fits their needs. The following checklist will help you to know your audience better, so that you can communicate more successfully:

- Who will your audience members be?
- What careers, fields, or interests do they represent?
- Why are they attending?
- What do they *know* about the subject?
- What is their *interest* in the subject?
- What is their relationship to you?
- What do they share in common: occasion, affiliation, profession, common interests, personal or professional goals?

Once you have gathered that information and thought it through, the answers to these further questions will give you the detailed information you need to make your presentation more relevant to your audience's needs and interests:

- What can you say that will be of most use or interest to participants?
- What can you say about how well they perform the task you are there to discuss?
- What other positive points can your talk include?
- How can you let the audience know you are sincere and realistic?
- How else can you help them see the benefits of your message?

When you wish to put a major effort into designing and delivering the best program possible outside your organization, you should seek the host group's support to help you gather the information suggested by the following checklist. This input will help considerably to ensure that you fulfill the organization's needs and those of the audience.

CHECKLIST

Audience

- Who are they?

  _____

- What is the makeup of the audience?

  _____

- How many will attend?

  _____

- How do they happen to be attending?

  _____

- What do they share in common?

  _____

- What do they *know* about the subject?

  _____

- What is their *interest* in the subject?

  _____

- What is their relationship to you?

  _____

- What do they share in common? (Please describe)

  Occasion _____

  Affiliation _____

Profession _____

Common Interests _____

Personal/Professional Goals _____

• What do you perceive as the main purpose of this presentation?

_____ Inform?

_____ Persuade? If so, in what context? _____

_____ Solve problems? Which ones? _____

_____ Arrive at decisions? Please specify: _____

Knowing Who or What Precedes and Follows You

Knowing as much about your speaking engagement as possible will help you to know your audience better. It will help you fit your presentation to their needs. Here are some questions you should have someone answer for you:

What precedes you?

You need to know what your audience will be doing before your presentation so that you can tailor your words and pace accordingly. Here are some general observations:

If you are the first speaker in the morning, you will want to use short sentences and keep a fresh "good morning" approach. If you follow a long meeting, you will have to be brief and upbeat. If you follow a break, you will have to be engaging to get them back on track. If you follow a meal, you will need to do your best to involve them. If you are the last speaker of the day, or if you follow a boring speaker, you will need to be as entertaining as possible. Again, brevity will earn extra points.

What follows you?

Know what takes place, or what your audience is scheduled to do after you finish. Try to find opportunities to bridge over to the next speaker or event.

How many people will be present?

Audience size often sets the level of formality for your talk. With large audiences, you will lecture more. Work to keep large audiences involved through rhetorical questions, similes and metaphors, appropriate humor, and other devices.

With smaller audiences, consider interspersing as much interaction, as much give and take, as possible. Make them part of the "show" where you can. Talk *with* them even more than you might talk *at* them.

Take into Account When You Are Speaking

Time is also an important factor: You will want to know how much time you have been allotted for your talk, and how much of it you should reserve for audience questions or participation. You will also want to consider how even the day of the week and time of day can help you tailor your message even further. If you have the ear of the meeting planner, here are some points to keep in mind and possibly share.

Mondays start the workweek, and many people write off Mondays as a matter of course. If you can avoid Monday presentations, do so. However, if you can't, you might want to try these tips: Relate to your audience members' weekend. That's possibly where their heads are anyway. Acknowledge the difficulty that many experience having to attend a meeting with a full week's work ahead of them. Hint that you intend to be brief. Don't say "I'll try not to be too long," but rather, "I have just three points to cover this morning." Keeping in mind the previous pointers given for the various types of audience members, lean toward a lighter, less pedantic style, stretching just to the edge of what the participants might consider acceptable style.

Fridays are also not desirable because people are already thinking about the weekend. If you're stuck with a Friday presentation—especially if it's in the afternoon—adapt the advice for Monday presentations.

On Tuesdays, the week is still young, and people are fresh and creative. They are also more likely to be receptive to new information and ideas, and to meetings that address problems.

Wednesdays are midweek and offer no special advantages or drawbacks in my estimation, having attended meetings for more than a quarter-century. If possible, try to gauge whether people might be "coming" or "going" in terms of the workweek. Are they still getting into their work load, or are they just starting to dig out from under it?

Thursdays are good meeting days when your purpose is to review familiar information, or to raise matters that can be concluded or decided. The week is far enough along, so that participants have been able to get much of their regular work done, and can thus concentrate on your message.

Mornings are better than afternoons because people are more alert and responsive. Avoid making presentations right after lunch. Research has shown that people are less attentive then. If you *must* speak between noon and 2:00 or 2:30, suggest postponing lunch until you conclude. However, if all else fails, offer coffee, turn up the lights, turn down the heat, and work hard to keep the audience engaged.

The best time to speak is 10:00 A.M. because by then people in organizations have checked their mail and messages and are generally ready to take a break from their routines.

When you are scheduled to speak, you will also want to know what format your program is expected to follow. Will it be a demonstration, a small-group conference, a workshop, a panel discussion, or a lecture, or will it follow some other format? Are you there to inform, motivate, or persuade? These matters will be covered in considerable detail later in this book.

8
Understanding Audiences

Whether you are a veteran speechwriter or are about to write your first speech, this new look at an old tool, Abraham Maslow's "Hierarchy of Needs," can help you evaluate your audience, tailor your message more precisely, and achieve the outcome you want.

Every communication should routinely answer the basics of who, what, when, where, and why. A top-notch communicator also answers the audience's unspoken questions: "So what? Who cares? And, What's in it for me?" People's "hidden" questions are: "Why are you telling me this? Why should I want to listen? And, how will my life (job, etc.) be better for having listened?"

To address these questions, you need to know your audience. As the previous chapter mentioned, audience profiles will vary in many respects, and you should always tailor your message to the demographics of each audience.

How to Motivate an Audience

Maslow isolated five levels of motivation in people and maintained that individuals must satisfy each level before they can advance to the next. At the most basic level, we have the survival needs of food, clothing, sleep, and so on. At level two, we have safety needs, including security, comfort, neatness, and order. At level three, we have all the belonging needs, such as membership, acceptance, and participation. Level four addresses the ego-status needs, such as recognition, achievement, and competency. At level five, we deal with self-actualization—doing things for the challenge, creativity, and esthetics that they involve.

MASLOW'S HIERARCHY OF NEEDS				
I. Basic	II. Safety	III. Belonging	IV. Esteem	V. Self-Actualization
Hunger	Security	Affiliation	Leadership	Fulfillment of potential
Thirst	Safety	Sharing	Achievement	Doing things for the challenge they offer
Sleep	Protection	Affection	Recognition	Intellectual stimulation
Health	Comfort	Acceptance	Confidence	Creativity
Physical well-being	Stability	Participation	Competence	Aesthetics
Sex	Neatness	Membership	Intelligence	Acceptance of reality

Psychologist Abraham H. Maslow studied thousands of people at varying success levels in their fields. He found that people must satisfy specific needs at given levels of motivation before they could advance to the next level—and that having satisfied a particular level, motivated individuals strive toward the higher levels still before them.

Having observed audiences for more than 25 years, I believe that most audience members tend to function at a solid level three on Maslow's scale while they are listening to your message. As the accompanying chart illustrates, just being part of an audience makes this possible—especially the membership, sharing, and participation aspects.

Thus, if your talk builds on their sense of belonging, your audience is already well on the way to accepting your message. You have established an emotional base with them—a rapport.

From there, you will select a need from Maslow's level four that is appropriate to the occasion and can appeal to your audience at that level. Level four includes such needs as leadership and achievement, recognition, confidence, competence, success, strength (physical or emotional), and intelligence.

Finding the "hot button" from level four and appealing to it specifically will help persuade the audience to accept your premises. Here is why: Maslow says that motivated individuals (audiences are at least motivated enough to attend your presentation) automatically seek gratification at the next level, once the present level is fulfilled.

In a rudimentary form, your motivators might go something like this: First, you address your audience at Maslow level three: "I'm glad that you are here today to participate in this program and to share in the ideas it has to offer." Then you let them know where your words will lead them in terms of Maslow level four: "The information you acquire here will help you to improve your leadership skills."

Naturally, this is only the skeleton, the rough outline for the content of your final presentation, but it gives you an idea of how the technique works. Not all individuals within an audience will be at a solid level three in every presentation. A small percentage of them may be fulfilled through level four, leaving level five as the only one to which you can appeal. A very few may even seem to have satisfied their needs at the highest level—level five.

When you communicate with such individuals, you will still need to address them at that level—at least in that particular situation—since it is highly unlikely that anyone has fulfilled each of these needs to his or her total satisfaction. However, if you feel you need to appeal to a still higher need, you might address their desire to help others, or to give back a measure of what life has given them.

Most audiences will respond well to speakers whose words implicitly acknowledge their needs to feel secure, to belong, to be presented with an opportunity, to advance, to be recognized, and to contribute to society. However, needs' levels vary throughout people's careers and personal lives. Sometimes, they will even vary from situation to situation, or from group to group.

In fact, even success at a given level can cause people to revert to a lower level. Take, for example, executives who receive promotions—and transfers. They may have been functioning at a Maslow four the day they learned of their promotion and transfer, then find themselves the next week in a strange city looking for new affiliations. They may even have to deal with temporarily uncomfortable living arrangements. Thus, for a while, they may have to function at least part-way without completely satisfying even their Maslow one needs.

If your objective were to sell a product or service to such individuals, you'd be wise to know and respect their Maslow level before proceeding. For example, there's not much sense trying to sell a self-improvement course (level four) to people who don't even know where or when they will be eating their next meal (level one). At that stage, they're a better prospect for a restaurant that can satisfy whatever needs they associate with food at the moment—homey atmosphere, speed, convenience, comfort, and quiet are just a few of the possibilities.

In one of my day-long seminars, a participant returned a phone call to her office during a break and was told that her house had been broken into. Fortunately, she was also told that nothing had been stolen and that her husband was taking care of things at home. There was no need for her to leave the seminar. She remained, but from that moment on, her mind functioned at a Maslow level two, as well it might. She was rightfully concerned for the safety and security of her home. It was almost impossible for her to give her full attention to the program. That would have been true of any program on any subject at that moment—unless, of course, the topic dealt with new security systems for the home.

Adapting to Audience Size and Stature

To become a better communicator, recognize that any Maslow level could contain a motivator that appeals to your listeners or readers. The higher the status of the group, the higher their Maslow level will generally be. Adapt your presentation accordingly. I do this almost automatically in my own seminars and one-on-one coaching sessions. For example, unlike most level three audiences, presidents and CEOs generally function at levels four or five; many trainees who are going through an orientation program—especially if they are entry-level, brand-new, or recently relocated—may be at a level two, or even one.

Of course, there are exceptions. A CEO brought me back for additional counsel when bad news was about to strike, and he felt that his firm was on the brink of disaster. Although he had clearly been at a Maslow level five a few months before, he was now concerned about level four issues, which meant that I needed to determine whether he was even solid at level three for the moment.

It turned out that, for himself, he was, but for his employees, he was concerned about their Maslow two needs—mostly in terms of their job security. For the session to succeed, we had to build all of his content around that issue, as I worked with him, personally, at a Maslow level three and began stretching him back toward level four. Clearly, the crisis would have to be resolved—which it was—and his employees would have to be secure again in their positions—which they ultimately were—before he could start thinking about Maslow five issues once more.

The point is to learn as much as you can about each audience, so that you can determine the level at which they have satisfied most or all of their needs. Then, focus your communication according to whatever you have to offer at the next level.

Recognize, too, that the larger the group, the more likely they are to be at a Maslow level three. When you address small groups, say of ten people or fewer, the Maslow levels of individuals will become more evident. You will have to fine tune and tailor accordingly.

Consider the motivators under each heading in the accompanying chart and ask yourself how you might use this information to address your participants' needs more closely?

Speaking Their "Language"

Before you start to write, you should also consider an audience's "representational systems"—how they receive and process information. At various times, people will tend to rely more heavily on one or another of their senses for this purpose. Generally, they will employ their visual, auditory, or kinesthetic (tactile) sense in a given situation. In a conversation, you can readily determine which sense they are using at the moment just by listening to their choice of verbs:

WHAT AUDIENCES REMEMBER

A note of irony lies behind all the preparing you will do for any presentation: According to one widely accepted set of figures, the average member of any audience will forget 80 percent of what you said by the end of a week. However, when you address your audience members' needs by speaking to the questions that are most relevant to them, you will help to boost their recall. Some of the questions that follow will be appropriate in specific situations, such as a problem-solving meeting; others will apply to presentations in general.

According to generally accepted figures, audience members forget:

40 percent of what they've just heard after 20 minutes.

60 percent of what they've just heard after a half day.

90 percent of what they've just heard after a week.

Each time you consider your audience, look through this list and select the questions that your audiences are most likely to be asking themselves when you present your points, proposals, or programs.

Purpose

Why is this necessary or desirable?

What can we expect it to accomplish?

How can it be implemented?

Who will be affected by it?

Where will this lead us?

How does it fit into our operations?

Concerns

Are there any drawbacks?

What difficulties or problems might it overcome? Create?

Will it be simple or difficult to operate or carry out?

What are its possible disruptive effects?

Cost (Time, Money, Staff)

How much will it cost?

Is that cost reasonable?

Can it pay for itself?

Where will the money come from?

How much time and energy might be required?

Who will carry it out?

Will it save time or money?

Benefits
> What are some of the advantages?
> What are its possible long-range benefits or results?
> Will it yield results or benefits quickly?

Acceptance
> Why is this good?
> Will others go along with the idea?
> Whom does it affect?
> Who supports or opposes the idea?
> What is at stake for these people?

Timing
> When should this be initiated?
> Is there a particularly good or bad time?
> Is there an essential starting or finishing date?
> What interim deadlines might be involved?
> At what stages will money be needed? How much?

- A visual processor might say, "I see."
- A person relying on auditory might say, "Sounds good."
- A tactile person might say, "I can handle that."

When you need to communicate with groups, rather than individuals, you can still use this tool. Audiences tend to respond favorably to visual verbs. Since speeches, themselves, require using the auditory sense, you can help your audiences process your information better by delivering your message with an abundance of visual predicates—and some tactile ones.

For years behaviorally oriented communicators have known that audiences retain only a small percentage of what they hear, a larger percentage of what they see and hear, and an even larger percentage of what they see, hear, and do. This is logical because it engages all three representational systems. Even if you can't involve your audience physically, you can benefit from using tactile verbs.

It may sound strange to focus on these two techniques—an audience's Maslow level and its representational systems—before you write. However, once you try it, you'll do it forever. Knowing your audience well before you begin to write will help you develop the most effective approach to your content.

DALE'S CONE OF EXPERIENCE
A researcher named Edgar Dale developed what is now known as "Dale's Cone of Experience." In this paradigm, Dale says that people generally remember:
20 percent of what they hear.
30 percent of what they see.
50 percent of what they hear and see.
80 percent of what they hear, see, and do.

Additional Tools for Recall

When you are trying to convey new information—a prime task in most presentations—it helps to know some of the "rules" that will make it easier for people to learn what you are there to convey.

Essentially, conveying information is a five-step process. You must succeed at each level to achieve the outcome you seek.

1. The information must be sent.
2. It must be received.
3. It must be understood.
4. It must be accepted.
5. It must be acted upon.

Adults, in particular, learn best when you help them proceed from agreement to uncertainty, from the known to the unknown. The stronger you can make the bridge between the two sets of extremes, the more likely your audience will be to accept the message.

Adults also learn better when, as a presenter, you:

- Explain your goals for them.
- Describe the steps they will need to take, or be asked to take, to achieve the goals you have set forth.
- Tell them how they will know when they are successful at each level and overall.
- Use yourself as a role model for good performance.
- Provide information that is related to their needs and interests.
- Give them opportunities to participate through discussion, role play, or other means.
- Establish a supportive, nonthreatening environment for learning.

Here is an effective and simple eight-step formula you can use whenever you need to convey new information:

1. Introduce the material.
2. Demonstrate it.
3. Discuss it.
4. Try it out through role play, especially through presentations designed to impart training in knowledge or skills.
5. Provide a way for participants to test what they learned.
6. Give them constructive feedback.
7. Make it okay for them not to know all the answers.
8. Move ahead only when they are ready.

9
Preparing Your Message

You wouldn't accept an invitation to speak unless you had something to say. Even knowledge, however, is not enough. You also need to decide what your purpose should be. Is it to inform? To solve problems? To arrive at decisions? Or is it to persuade? (And persuasion is the bottom line of most presentations.) Once you know your purpose, you will be even better prepared to start writing your talk.

The Need for Brevity and Simplicity

Before we discuss writing, however, there is an important point to keep in mind: Television has set the standards for communication in today's society. We live in a fast-food-information world in which consumers expect that every product will be stripped to the bones, processed, and packaged before it is fed to them in easily consumed bites.

Within this very generation, people were willing to listen to a speaker for an hour. Today, even a member of the clergy has to limit his or her message to 20 minutes or less. Again, television creates our expectations: Interviews on talk shows once ran 15 minutes. Now they rarely last more than seven to ten minutes. Television interviewers used to allow a guest the luxury of a one-minute response. About ten years ago, that had diminished to about 45 seconds. By 1988, an interviewer was likely to interrupt a guest, or the camera was likely to cut back to the interviewer, once the answer had run 25 seconds.

The message to presenters? Be brief or lose your audience. Deliver your presentation in short, easy-to-follow segments.

Gathering Facts

Before you try to write out your message, collect all the random facts you might want to include. Arranging them to meet your audience's needs comes later. Begin your "shopping list" by gathering and jotting down as many random ideas on the subject as you feel might be useful. Don't even question their validity.

The age-old technique of "brainstorming" comes in handy here, and you can use it alone if you follow this approach: Examine your audience profile, and then write the first fact that comes to mind. Now look at that fact, and write down your very next thought. Don't question it. Don't judge it. Just write it down.

To prompt your thought processes, say things to yourself, such as: "When I look at the words _____," (which you just wrote down), "it makes me think of _____ _____," (and write down your very next thought).

"Chunking"

Once you have listed 100 or more ideas, facts, phrases, and thought starters, consider how you can cluster them. Behavior-communications people call this "chunking." It should be your first step in assembling the information your audience needs, in a way that they can remember.

The rule of chunking says that people recall the most information when the presenter limits his or her talk to seven chunks of information, plus or minus two. To be safe, then, you will want no more than five clusters. Three, for reasons we will see later, would be even more effective.

The concept of chunking was developed by G. A. Miller, who called it the "magical number seven, plus or minus two," in a paper on the limits to our capacity to process information.

Chunking helps to unify fragments of information into like quantities. This helps to avoid a problem that is even more serious—overload.

With each idea you introduce in a speech, you compound the risk that your audience will forget or confuse what they have heard. This is partly because people sort ideas in terms of other ideas they have previously heard. They do not simply accept each new bit of information in pure, linear fashion. For example, if you present just one idea, that is all they have to remember:

A

However, life is rarely that simple. Let's consider what happens when you present two separate pieces of information:

A-B   B-A

So far, so good. Two ideas can only be presented in two different ways. However, as you read on, it will help you to remember that the listener's mind can (and will) attend to, check, and cross-check information in as many ways as it can be presented—regardless of the sequence in which you may present each thought.

Consequently, three pieces of information create a total of six different ways of presenting or processing:

A-BC	B-AC	C-AB
A-CB	B-CA	C-BA

Thus far, readers or listeners should be able to sort, re-sort, and recall—with reasonable accuracy—this number of topics. However, the complexity begins once you reach four major ideas. With four, the audience has to sort through 24 potential combinations and try to retain what it can.

A-BCD	B-ACD	C-ABD	D-ABC
A-BDC	B-ADC	C-ADB	D-ACB
A-CBD	B-CAD	C-BAD	D-BAC
A-CDB	B-CDA	C-BDA	D-BCA
A-DBC	B-DAC	C-DAB	D-CAB
A-DCB	B-DCA	C-DBA	D-CBA

When you get up to five major thoughts or topics, the combinations begin to become overwhelming. Yet articles or presentations often contain five—or more—separate and distinct ideas of equal "weight." Consider an annual report or a speech at an annual meeting, for example.

At five major thoughts, the audience experiences serious overload—a possible 120 different ways to juggle your information:

A-BCDE	B-ACDE	C-ABDE	D-ABCE	E-ABCD
A-BCED	B-ACED	C-ABED	D-ABEC	E-ABDC
A-BDCE	B-ADCE	C-ADBE	D-ACBE	E-ACBD
A-BDEC	B-ADEC	C-ADEB	D-ACEB	E-ACDB
A-BECD	B-AECD	C-AEBD	D-AEBC	E-ADBC
A-BEDC	B-AEDC	C-AEDB	D-AECB	E-ADCB

A-CBDE	B-CADE	C-BADE	D-BACE	E-BACD
A-CBED	B-CAED	C-BAED	D-BAEC	E-BADC
A-CDBE	B-CDAE	C-BDAE	D-BCAE	E-BCAD
A-CDEB	B-CDEA	C-BDEA	D-BCEA	E-BCDA
A-CEBD	B-CEAD	C-BEAD	D-BEAC	E-BDAC
A-CEDB	B-CEDA	C-BEDA	D-BECA	E-BDCA
A-DBCE	B-DACE	C-DABE	D-CABE	E-CABD
A-DBEC	B-DAEC	C-DAEB	D-CAEB	E-CADB
A-DCEB	B-DCAE	C-DBAE	D-CBAE	E-CBAD
A-DCBE	B-DCEA	C-DBEA	D-CBEA	E-CBDA
A-DEBC	B-DEAC	C-DEAB	D-CEAB	E-CDAB
A-DECB	B-DECA	C-DEBA	D-CEBA	E-DCBA
A-EBCD	B-EACD	C-EABD	D-EABC	E-DABC
A-EBDC	B-EADC	C-EADB	D-EACB	E-DACB
A-ECBD	B-ECAD	C-EBAD	D-EBAC	E-DBAC
A-ECDB	B-ECDA	C-EBDA	D-EBCA	E-DBCA
A-EDBC	B-EDAC	C-EDAB	D-ECAB	E-DCAB
A-EDCB	B-EDCA	C-EDBA	D-ECBA	E-DCBA

You do not need to be a mathematician to notice that the possibilities are increasing exponentially. We are now dealing with equations, not just simple numbers, and this exercise examines only what happens with the main points. It doesn't even consider how the subtopics or subordinate points affect the calculations—not to mention the audience's brains.

How can knowing this help us communicate more effectively? By calling to mind an "ancient" piece of advice that has survived the generations: The "KISS" formula, which we edit slightly for our own use. When you write or speak, *K*eep *I*t *S*hort and *S*imple.

Your Next Step

Once you have listed all the points you will be covering, try to find what they have in common, and then sort them into three clusters. Some might not be a perfect "fit," but do the best you can. The next step in the process will take care of any misfits.

Next, decide which cluster should be last. This will generally be the most complicated, the most complex, or the most specialized or technical. Arrange the information in that cluster in the most logical sequence possible. Then decide which cluster should precede it by asking yourself what the flow of information should be. Now sequence that cluster.

Finally, decide which cluster should go first. This will generally be the cluster that contains the information that is easiest to present or understand, the one with the most common denominator, or the one that has the broadest base for your foundation. Sequence that cluster next.

Now, with all your raw data entered into a word processor, put your "chunks" into three files. Label the first one "ending," and put the material you plan to use in your ending into it. Label the second one "middle," and put the content that will go into your speech's middle into it. Label the third "beginning," and put all the points you plan to use in your beginning into that one.

At the top of the ending file, type in the word ending and the ending you have chosen as your primary one. Do the same with the middle and beginning files.

Next, within each file, move your notes, points, or thoughts around, so that they cluster together naturally. The process is much like that followed by efficient shoppers at the supermarket. Starting with a random list, they put similar things into categories according to where things are located in their store. For example, they "chunk" all canned goods together, all dairy items together, all produce together, all meats together, all frozen items together, all toiletries together, and so on.

Next, an efficient shopper recognizes how the store is laid out and arranges each cluster of items accordingly. While it might seem sensible to start at one end of the store and work down each aisle, that approach is not the wisest. Why pick up perishables (such as fresh produce), cooler items (such as milk, eggs, meats), and frozen food before loading the cart with the canned goods, paper products, and the like? Why put heavy items, such as canned goods, on top of fragile products?

Bottom-line thinking comes into play as the shopper asks, "What category of items do I want to put in the cart *last?* In what sequence should I load *those* in? What should go in before that group?" and so on. If you follow the same kind of thinking as you arrange your notes within each file, you will have your material in order before you ever put it in sentence form.

Beginnings, Middles, and Endings

David Campbell's book, *If You Don't Know Where You're Going, You'll Probably End Up Somewhere Else,* stands out among many others in my office. It reminds me that even when we communicate, we must have a goal, a bottom line, and a destination.

There's another good reason for focusing this way: Throughout my career, I have found that many of the executives who will have the power of thumbs-up or thumbs-down over one's proposals tend to be "bottom-line" oriented—particularly when they listen to others' presentations. You might as well anticipate this and let it guide your planning.

Backing into the Best Start

Most professional communicators begin with a wealth of information about their topic. As they look through their research or notes, they begin to consider how to organize it. They approach their presentations from the front end of the job, starting with the beginning. To me, this is much like trying to push a piece of wet spaghetti across a table: It's much easier to go around to the other side of the table, the destination, and pull it across.

When I became aware of this several years ago, I developed a way to speed up any writing task and help you reach your objective. It's called "Organizing Words from End to Beginning ©," and here is why it works:

Good communicators begin by considering the bottom line. They ask: "What do I want to leave my audience with?" (And, yes, even professional communicators end thoughts with prepositions.) Writers and speakers realize that to succeed, they have to know where they're headed. This is true throughout life. To draw an analogy, you don't plan a trip to Cape Cod by asking yourself how to get out of the driveway. You begin by saying, "I want to go to Cape Cod." This is your destination, your goal, your objective. From this knowledge, you can begin to think about how to reach that goal, which route to take, so to speak.

The same holds true when you develop a speech or a presentation. You should think first of the destination—call it the ending or bottom line. The question to raise is: "What is the most important way to close?" Once you have fixed on that goal, it becomes much easier—using the end-to-beginning approach—to develop the proper "route" or middle for your talk—which route to take, and why. Having done that, you will find that the beginning—the "How-do-I-get-out-of-my-driveway?" part of writing—will take care of itself, and you can deal with it later.

"Organizing Words from End to Beginning ©" discusses the five ways with which to conclude a message, five kinds of middles, and five kinds of beginnings. The system works for any oral or written communication. You start by selecting the kind of ending that best suits your purpose. Next, you consider which kind of middle best flows into your ending. Finally, you select the kind of beginning that leads most logically into your middle.

Five Types of Endings

The first step in the end-to-beginning approach should be to look over your material and ask yourself, "What is the most important or logical way to end this communication? How do I want to conclude?" Here are the five kinds of endings from which you can select. You can:

1. *Summarize.* Giving your audience a succinct restatement of the ideas you will expand on in your middle.
2. *Relate your ending to your beginning.* You have not written a beginning yet, but you will. Some call this a "full-circle" ending.
3. *Outline a plan.* Giving the audience specific steps you might want them to follow. Some call this a "plan-of-action" ending.
4. *Tell why the particular plan you outlined is best.* This kind of ending goes beyond just concluding with a plan to persuade the reader to adopt the plan (which will most likely be outlined in your middle when you use this kind of ending).
5. *Show how your words have value and meaning to your audience.* This answers the readers' or listeners' unspoken questions, including "What's in it for me?" "Why should I?" And so on.

Pick the kind of ending that works best for your audience, your situation, your topic, and your intentions. In special cases, such as lengthy or complex communications, you may want to add elements of another type of ending. Just be sure to emphasize your primary choice.

Once you have selected the kind of ending you want, use your notes to develop it into a rough draft. You can then consider your middle.

Five Types of Middles

Of the five kinds of middles available, select one that best leads into the ending you have drafted. Here are the five types:

1. *Topical.* Lists facts point by point, subject by subject, as part of a whole concept.
2. *Spatial.* Emphasizes the physical order or sequence in which things happen, helping the reader to follow along.
3. *Problem/Solution.* Tells the audience what is wrong and how the problem might be remedied. This can also take such forms as Question–Answer, Cause–Effect, or Pro–Con.
4. *Time.* Organizes facts in chronological sequence.
5. *Reason.* Explains the logic behind what you are saying.

Draft your middle, and then consider which of the five kinds of beginnings will best lead your audience into it. As you consider endings and middles, you may think about how you will begin. This is fine, as long as you leave the design and phrasing of your beginning to last.

Thus far, you have controlled your destination, or ending, by selecting it in advance. You have controlled your route, or middle, by working backward, step by step. Now, it should be easy to "get out of your driveway"—to write those often difficult first words.

Look over your notes again and, from the information remaining, select those facts that will help you write a solid beginning. You don't need to use all that are left, or you may have to develop a few more, or you may also have to "borrow" one or two from your middle or, more likely, from your ending.

Five Types of Beginnings

1. *State the subject area in general terms.* For example, in a report on sales in a specific state, you might start with an overview of the region.
2. *Start with a specific part of the subject.* You might begin by writing about sales of pencils, and then broaden to sales of all office supplies.
3. *Compare an unrelated topic to your subject.* This is useful when your audience knows little about your subject, but might understand it better if you compare it to something with which they are familiar. For instance, you might compare racquetball to tennis if the audience is already familiar with the latter sport.
4. *Discuss the background for your topic.* This is sometimes called a "stage-setter" beginning. For example, to oppose tearing down an important monument, you might begin by talking about why it was originally erected.

5. *Use the reason for your message as your beginning.* This kind of beginning answers such questions as "Why this message, why this audience, and why this occasion."

Pick the kind of beginning that works best for you, and write it. Now review the entire draft in the traditional sequence, from beginning to end. Edit it to make it easier for the reader or listener to follow, and do whatever else you can to improve your message. Because you knew where you were headed before you started out, your task as a communicator will have been that much easier.

Note: We began writing this section by selecting a *full-circle* ending, which contains some elements of *value and meaning.* After that we developed a *topical* middle and arranged it in *spatial* order. Then we prepared a *specific-part* beginning.

An Illustration

Here is how one of our industrial clients applied the system. Put yourself in his place, so that you will experience what it is like to think your way through the process, regardless of your topic.

The firm is located in a town that is becoming concerned with industrial pollution of its waterways. The company's president senses a "lynch mob" attitude developing and asks you to write a position statement that managers can use to discuss this problem with the press, local officials, and the general public.

For starters, you know that your company, as a responsible "good neighbor," has taken specific and costly steps to clean up the water your plant discharges into a local river. You will certainly want to tell your audience about the steps that your firm has taken and will continue to take. In fact, a summary might be the best way. How did we arrive at that decision? By process of elimination, we can cross off (3), a "project-plan" type, because you are not trying to tell the public what to do. This also eliminates ending (4) that "tells them why the plan you outlined is best." To end by relating what you have said to your introduction (2) works best when you want to close with one specific point, so this is also out. You could show the audience why your words have value and meaning to them (5), but in this case, it might be better to be less forceful.

Following the same deductive logic we used to select an ending, you narrow down the choices to one middle. Topical (1) is out because you are not listing qualities as parts of a whole. Spatial (2) is of little use because it is not your objective to arrange ideas in a logical sequence or locate specific objects in a "geographic" sequence. Problem-solution (3) and reason (5) require various forms of argumentation that might not be desirable here. That leaves time (4) as the most suitable type of middle in this case.

Why? Because you are trying to discuss your company's efforts to prevent polluted water from being discharged into the local river. In this case, you also know that the company took many of these steps well ahead of the public awareness of the growing need to prevent water pollution, and years ahead of any local or state regulations requiring preventive devices or procedures.

But, you might ask, will you not also want to discuss a particular process for filtering wastes? And will this not lead into a spatial middle (from machine through pipes, filters, settlement tanks, purifier, and finally through discharge pipes)? Of course. And this is logical. Every speech has one main method of organization with perhaps another or more at work in subordinate roles throughout.

For instance, you might want to show that your firm has been reclaiming much of the previously discharged waste and selling it or reusing it in other ways to reduce costs. Economists might call this enlightened self-interest. Whatever you call it, it is a sound argument for the way your firm will continue to keep pace with ways to reduce waste.

The argument might go like this: "We studied the problem, discussed the facts, concluded that we could reduce and reclaim waste, tried various approaches, found that the XYZ Process works best, approved the plan, and installed the equipment. The result? Cleaner water and cost savings in processing our product. Thus, you may be certain that we will continue working to prevent water pollution. Doing so is in our common interest."

This gives you a subordinate middle that combines both the problem-solution and reason methods. It could have taken a different form, combining the same methods, if you had said: "We have 2,000 families represented in our plant and nearly 85 percent of them live in attractive homes in this community. We are concerned that their water supply remain pure because if it doesn't, our employees will move." Again, enlightened self-interest, but a convincing argument, nevertheless.

The next step within the time method is to determine what to say and in what sequence to say it. This will depend on your company's history on this issue. Essentially, you will follow the calendar or the clock. But, even then, you will find yourself amplifying on the specific products, procedures, or processes you instituted at each juncture. Just select what is important to support your case and organize it accordingly. Ultimately, you will have a middle that is well-illustrated with examples and statistics.

Now let's see how you might begin your presentation. You would not want to start with a *specific segment* (2) because you would have to extract it from your time method of organization. You could *start with another subject and compare* (3), if you feel your audience knows little about your subject and needs the comparison to understand it. But this is not the case here. Nor would you need to *discuss the background to your topic* (4)—the audience already knows why you are talking about pollution. Finally, you could use the *reason for your speech* (5) as a point from which to begin: "The Citizen's Committee for Clean Water has asked our support of Water Conservation Bill No. 523 now before the Senate. We recognize the value of this bill and encourage all employees to let their elected officials know of their desire to see this proposal passed. Our company also supports this proposal."

Still, the best choice seems to be to *state the subject area in general terms* (1), introducing the steps the firm has taken: "The ABC Company has taken several steps to prevent water pollution." You want to let the community know what steps you have taken and plan to take to prevent water pollution. Thus, statement of the subject area—in which you prepare your audience for what follows—is the type of beginning that will best communicate the desired message in this case.

Your next step would be to write out the end, middle, and beginning, rearrange the sequence from beginning to end, and add whatever transitions you might need as you read it through.

The Power of Threes

People will accept and recall the points in your next presentation better if you speak in threes—three words, three numbers, or three topics, for example. These triads, clusters of things in threes, are more familiar to us than we might realize.

Think about such well-known phrases as: "Duty, God, and country," "Faith, hope, and charity," or even, "Up, up, and away!" Now try adding a fourth element to each one. Notice what happens when you say them out loud. Try these: "Duty, God, country, and friends." Or "Faith, hope, charity, and kindness." Or how about, "Up, up, away, and gone!" Clearly, something suffers.

Try a few more. Consider: "I came. I saw. I conquered." Think what would happen had you said, "I came. I saw. I battled. Then I conquered." How about turning "Friends, Romans, countrymen . . . lend me your ears," into "Friends, Romans, countrymen, and strangers. . . ." Finally, imagine how it would sound if Gertrude Stein had not said, "A rose, is a rose, is a rose," but rather, "A rose, is a rose, is a rose—is a rose." In each case, something gets lost—rhythm, meter, and power.

A phone number has three parts: area code, prefix, and last four digits. Traffic signals have three lights: red, amber, and green. There are three primary colors: red, blue, and yellow. To start a race, we often say, "On your mark, get set, go." To entice children to jump into the water, adults frequently say, "One, two, three." The examples are endless.

In fact, the triad concept is all around us. We speak of "morning, noon, and night" although there's no special reason for including noon. If asked, most people would say it just "sounds" better.

Similarly, it also sounds better for a presentation to have a beginning, middle, and end. The middle of a talk, itself, will be most effective when it is limited to three ideas.

What accounts for this magic of threes, this power of the triad? Clearly, it works, and the reason may come down to something as simple as this: If you present information in ways that are familiar to an audience, they are more likely to understand it, accept it, and recall it. (And that's another triad.)

Building Acceptance for Your Position

Have you been getting "no" for an answer more than you might care to admit? Or, is your next presentation so critical that you would like to improve your technique for motivating people to agree with you? If so, here is a technique you might consider: Richard Sutphen calls it "creating the 'yes-set.'" It is a technique well-known to politicians and trial attorneys. In fact, Sutphen says that trial attorneys refer to it as "tightening the noose."

SETTING UP THE TECHNIQUE

You begin by creating what is known as a "yes-set." This consists of a series of three things with which your listeners will most likely agree. That is followed by three more statements (or questions) that could be debated, but that most listeners will accept—once they have already accepted the first three statements. Those are then followed by the point with which you ultimately want your listener to agree.

Since, as we saw, triads have a power of their own, this technique is even more persuasive because it is a three-step technique. In fact, even the beginning contains a three-part setup that is followed by a three-part middle, that is then followed with a powerful persuader.

Here's how the technique might work. Begin with three statements that elicit agreement:

1. "Are you tired of waiting hours each week for your turn to use the photocopier?"
2. "Do you feel that standing in lines is the best use of your time?"
3. "Are you annoyed with how you miss phone calls and visitors while you are making photocopies?"

Follow those with three statements that are reasonably acceptable:

1. "As you know all too well, getting secretarial or staff help to run these errands for you is no longer an option."
2. "Because of the recent cutback, the clerical help we have is already overburdened."
3. "Even their time has more value than we can justify allocating to standing in line for a copy machine."

Then you close with your persuasive statement: "The solution is not more staff, not more time, but something even more simple: an additional and inexpensive photocopier at either end of each floor, keeping the professional, heavy-duty model at the half-way point for use only when it is absolutely needed."

You now have their attention: Take them through a logical cost-benefits analysis that stresses savings in terms of costs-per-copy on the cheaper machines, as well as time, and you may get your copiers. I have seen this technique produce impressive results, especially when professional communicators I have coached to write editorials have used it—particularly in shareholder magazines.

Making Presentations "Sparkle"

As you develop your talk in detail, look for opportunities—particularly in your middle—to insert such "sparklers" as *appropriate* and *pertinent* quotes, examples, statistics, anecdotes, and humor. These and other devices will help you capture and retain the audience's interest.

There are other ways to add sparkle to the information you present. You can eliminate dull, wordy sentences that are hard to follow. With a little practice, you can also increase the power of your messages by removing all the "shun" verbs. These are the words that end in *sion* or *tion*. For example, why say, "The improvement resulted in the produc*tion* of . . . ," when you can say "The improvement produced . . . ?" Why say, "The manager gave considera*tion* to the proposal," when you can say "considered?"

To convert *shun* words into active verbs, you have to answer such questions as, "Who did what to whom?" To fill this need, you will have to use people's names or titles, and thus improve clarity. This, in turn, gives more useful information to the audience.

Here are some examples for you to work on. (Hint: Convert the *shun* words to active ones in each sentence, then edit.)

- Resumption of operations at all mines is expected Monday as a result of action based upon the union's decision.
- The recommendation will result in an extension in negotiations.
- The determination of the composition of the product will affect the quality of its distribution.
- In the conversation, he gave recognition to the fact that the book was subject to various interpretations.
- She worked in isolation but with appreciation with regard to the contributions of her peers.
- Please give some indication of the information we can use in the preparation of this report for publication.
- The project has been completed as far as excavation is concerned.

See how much more powerful each of these statements becomes when you strip out the "shun" words. You add immediacy, action, and even drama—and all three help to keep your audience members tuned in.

Passive Voice Dulls Speeches

You can also increase the power of your writing and improve audience acceptance when you speak in the active rather than the passive voice. Consider the discussion that follows—written largely in the passive voice—and see how dull it really is. Then see how you might improve the passage by making it as active as possible:

The passive voice shows that the subject is acted upon rather than performing the action. Use of the passive voice often results in unemphatic, vague, wordy, and indirect sentences. The active voice should be preferred because it is more direct, forceful, and vigorous. It encourages brevity as well as clarity.

However, at times the passive voice can be used effectively. For example, when the person who carries out an action is deemed to be of less importance than the outcome itself: "Smith was sent home early today." "The truck was backed right into the closed door on the loading dock."

The passive voice can also be used when it is not known who performed an action: "Business attire is considered quite flexible in today's society." "The commuter train was reported to be running about ten minutes late."

When the writer wishes to place the subject of the sentence at the end for emphasis, he or she might also use the passive voice: "The market can only be recaptured by aggressive retailing." "The turnaround was achieved by Chrysler."

When tact or restraint is important, the passive voice can also be effective: "The problems confronting that industry have been mitigated by the presence of a skilled negotiator." "It has been shown that proper application of these procedures can have an advantageous effect on the outcome of the process."

QUICK QUIZ

How many times can you find the passive voice in the preceding discussion. How can you rewrite this section to make it more vital? This is useful practice, especially since passive language tends to obscure meaning even more for listeners than it does for readers. Readers, at least, can reread phrases or even pages to try to find the correct context. Listeners have to try to keep up with the presenter's next words.

How to Use Humor

Putting humor in a presentation is no joking matter: To write and deliver it naturally can be a lot of work. Ask any speechwriter. It's one thing to be able to *see* the humor in a situation, writing it *into* a situation is considerably harder. To write humor for speeches, the writer must understand how to relate the funny story to the occasion, how it fits in with the specific topic, and how it will work with a specific audience. The writer must also make the story fit the speaker's personality and style, and must place it appropriately and effectively within the talk.

Omit any of these, and the punch line may fall flat. Further, when the humor is forced or squeezed, it often comes out distorted and loses its impact. It could even backfire.

Strained humor can be awkward and embarrassing for both speaker and audience. Presenters who struggle to make a bad joke work can consider themselves fortunate when it merely bombs. At the extreme are those speakers who believe they are "supposed to" open with "a few jokes," and then kill their audience by reading the stories right off the paper.

If humor is so difficult to write into a talk, if it is so difficult to deliver, and if it can have so many potentially negative consequences, why bother? Perhaps for these reasons: Used properly, humor can illustrate and underscore points through irony, contrast, and juxtaposition. It can entertain, reduce tension, and lighten a heavy topic.

MAKE IT "FIT"

Where should humor occur within a talk? There is no actual formula. Humor should arise when and where it fits—generally, to change the pace or to signal that change. Among the "rules," consider these: Humor should flow with the presentation, not interrupt it. Like the seasoning in a delicate dish, it should compliment the food, but never call attention to itself. It should be relevant, sincere, brief, inoffensive, and fresh. It should also be sparse. A few, well-chosen stories will go over much better than a dozen "jokes."

MAKE IT TIMELY

Humor needs to be timely, but don't try to rehash the most current "joke" making the rounds. Instead, try to address topical issues, using a line that people may have heard recently. For example, when I spoke before the American Society of Personnel Administrators' Annual Leadership Conference right after the 1988 Presidential Debates, I used this story to establish an early rapport with this audience of experienced presenters:

"Driving in this morning, I was trying to envision myself having the right professional attitude for this talk, and I was trying to come up with a role model to emulate. As an admirer of the Kennedy wit and style, I had just about decided to use *him* as my role model when I heard a voice inside my head that sounded strangely like Bentsen's say: 'But sir, you're no Jack Kennedy!' "

The story was a good ice-breaker because it was timely, yet familiar enough, and the joke was strictly on me. It helped me become more "human" to this audience of experienced presenters, and they appreciated it even more because they could empathize with me.

MAKE YOURSELF THE TARGET

If the joke has to be on someone, make it on you. When you do, the audience will be far more accepting and will more readily identify with you. This can ease any tension that might be present, and can also create a stronger rapport through empathy. The late President Kennedy was a master at this. When asked how he became a war hero, he replied: "It was absolutely involuntary—they sank my boat."

GIVE AND GAIN EMPATHY

Empathy is, indeed, important when using humor. Never use it to set someone up as a target, or to demean individuals or groups, or to create a "loser." It is better to make yourself the brunt of the joke than to insult someone—no matter how much you, or the audience, feel the individual "deserves" it.

Shortly after I moved to a "country" area in Virginia, I was the after-dinner speaker for a professional group in a major city. When the emcee (whom we'll call Ted Borten) introduced me, he made an unsuccessful stab at humor—describing my home in Fauquier County as "rural" in most uncomplimentary terms.

I could have responded with any number of "put-downs" such as: "It always helps to be introduced by someone like Ted Borten. Just looking at him reminds you of a joke." Of course, I didn't. Actually, the remark didn't surprise me. Many people whose organizations have scheduled my presentations and seminars know that I spent more than 25 years as an executive in New York City. Thus, it was only a matter of time before someone, somewhere, made a "country" reference to my new home when introducing me.

So, I smiled and said: "You know, Ted, speaking of the country life, I almost didn't *get* here this evening. We had quite a fire in the bathroom this morning. . . . We were lucky, though. It never reached the house!" Then, in the same breath, I turned my full attention to the audience and began my opening with a smile, even as they continued to chuckle.

DEVELOP YOUR RESOURCES

Where does humor come from? The obvious answer is from life itself. We need to ask: How can we develop our own sense of humor, so that we can dispense it at will, when and where appropriate?

Think about what makes *you* laugh. Write down the stories that give you the most pleasure. Ask yourself why, and write that down, too. Do the same with stories that make your friends and colleagues laugh. Avoid the books on clever introductions, humor for all occasions, and the like. Most of their stories are shopworn. Even the better ones read "funnier" than they sound when you try to deliver them. At best, you would have to overhaul them, make them conversational, and make the humor fit the point you wish to make.

Here's a simpler approach: Notice the humor that appears in the publications that you, your friends, and your associates read. Do the same with the publications your audience reads. Also, when something you happen to say spontaneously makes people laugh—or when someone else makes you laugh—write that down as well. Collect these stories, and sort them by category or subject. Soon you'll have all the stories you need, when you need them.

Is humor worth the effort? When it works, you bet—but preparing to use it well? That's no laughing matter. Preparing humor, like preparing any "sparkler," takes time. It takes research to find what you need, and it requires careful planning to integrate it into a presentation where it will do the most good.

Delivery? That's something else again, and would take us well beyond the scope of this book. You might want to check the references in the bibliography for guidance on this point.

Ten Dynamic Ways to Open

You have now chosen the type of opening for your speech, and selected the points you want to make in that opening. Next, you have to develop the best possible opening—one that will catch your audience's attention from the first words you speak.

There are basically ten ways to get the job done, according to a colleague of many years, Ronald N. Levy, President of North American Precis Syndicate, Inc., of New York City, Washington, and Chicago. You are bound to find one or two on this list that fits your audience, format, and topic.

1. *Question the Listener.* The objective here is to involve audience members in the process as quickly as possible. Example: "Do you have a good head for business? The hat industry believes you do. Americans spend more than $100 million on headgear annually."

2. *Open with an Historical Reference.* Avoid the trite: "It has been x years since . . . ," and say something, such as: "Ever since cavemen

learned that there's more than one way to skin a tiger, forms of education have varied."

3. *Offer the "Inside Story."* Let the audience know you are sharing facts to which few people are privy: "A new formula will enable plastic bottles and containers to disintegrate shortly after they are discarded. The secret ingredient? Cornstarch. Here's how scientists came up with the concept."

4. *Begin with a Rhyme or an Alliteration.* This captures the audience's fancy in an entertaining way, even as it builds suspense: "Rich man, poor man, beggar man, thief. They all have something in common—with each other, and with everyone in this room."

5. *Make a Prediction.* "By the turn of the century, more than 30 million people will be using a device that was little-known just a few years ago."

6. *Start with an Entertaining Sound.* "Thump! Thump! Thump! Thump! It happens over a hundred thousand times a day. Your heart gulps in a few ounces of blood, then pumps out a fresh supply."

7. *Begin with a Quote.* Since many speakers open this way, your best bet will be to avoid quotes that may be overly familiar to your audience. You can even paraphrase: "Today, we will talk about risk taking and, as we do, let us draw comfort from Schopenhauer's reminder that every new idea is first ridiculed, then vigorously attacked, then taken for granted."

8. *Start with a Pun.* People groan when they hear the punch line of a pun, but puns get audience's attention: "People are 'dye-ing' more these days, as the retail price of clothing has skyrocketed."

9. *"Even as We Speak."* Involve your audience members by providing a contrast between what they are doing, have done, or will be doing, and an event that relates to your topic: "During the time it takes us to inhale our next four breaths, x Americans are taking their last one."

10. *Make a Promise.* Appeal to participants' self-interest by offering a benefit right up front: "If the stress of daily commuting has gotten to you, the next 20 minutes will show you how to banish that concern—forever."

Not all of these leads will work in the business environments in which you speak. Some may be more appropriate for external, less formal audiences. However, you are bound to find at least one among these ten that will help you "grab" your audience when you open.

Now you have three files that contain end, middle, and beginning material. You have selected the type of end, middle, and beginning that will serve you best. You have reviewed all you know about your audience. You have dropped in your "sparklers" and developed the material into a logical flow of thoughts and sentences. You are ready to edit your first, rough draft. Save the three files and create an additional new one from them. Sequence this in the traditional way—beginning, middle, and ending.

What to Ask when You Proofread

As you look at your computer screen, you should see what is now becoming your talk. Before you print it out, you will need to edit it. Here is an editorial process that is effective and easy to follow. Just ask yourself these questions:

1. Have I put everything in proper form?
2. Have I eliminated the "mechanical" errors of punctuation, grammar, and spelling?
3. Do my nouns and verbs agree in number? Have I kept related words together, so that my meaning is clear?
4. Have I used nouns and verbs instead of adjectives and adverbs wherever possible?
5. Have I avoided overworked expressions?
6. Have I avoided abstractions by using examples, facts, and other concrete supporting material?
7. Have I used precise words, whether nouns or verbs?
8. Have I cut out all words, phrases, clauses, sentences, and even paragraphs that do not contribute to my message?
9. Have I combined like thoughts into single sentences wherever possible?
10. Are my sentences varied? Have I avoided careless repetition of words and sounds? Have I intermingled various kinds of sentence structures for variety? Have I varied the subject-verb order, as well as the position of modifiers and parenthetical elements?
11. Have I been cohesive? Have I used words or phrases that will ensure continuity both in structure and meaning?
12. Have I eliminated the passive voice and "shun" words wherever possible?
13. Have I been logical? Does one fact support the next? Does anything seem contradictory? Have I answered all questions that I may have raised?

14. Will my audience understand each expression or phrase? Have I supported any viewpoints with facts that they will understand?
15. Have I used "sparklers" effectively?
16. Does my conclusion logically follow from what I have said? Do I have a conclusion? Is it strong? Or have I trailed off or, worse, tacked on an ending that will weaken the content?
17. Does the presentation "tell itself?" Have I used others' views instead of my own where it would be more appropriate to do so?
18. Are my facts correct? Have I documented them or credited their sources?

Once you have addressed these concerns, you will have a manuscript in your computer, and you will be ready for the next step.

10
The Only Way to Prepare a Typescript

Now that you have a clean, proof-read manuscript in your computer, you are ready for the next step—one that will improve your delivery techniques beyond anything else you might have done. It will make you a better presenter forever.

I have used this technique with hundreds of clients, including the president of a major, privately held corporation, who initially opposed it. For the first half hour, we worked with a traditionally typed manuscript that he had not seen before. It had neat right-hand margins, double-spaced copy in a "speech" typeface, and the lines ran to the bottom of each page.

However, he was having difficulty reading it and could not look up without losing his place. He paused where there were no pauses and tripped over words that should have been familiar. Ruling out any other possible contributing factors, he needed two days with any new speech before he could deliver it.

Lacking that time, he agreed to set up the beginning according to the guidance offered here. Within 10 minutes we had that much of the text ready. Within another 10 minutes, he was delivering it like a professional platform speaker.

He liked the technique—so will you.

Adjusting Your Text

Your text is still in the computer, so once you're satisfied with it, print out a copy on plain 8½- × 11-inch paper. This is not your final draft. You will use it only to prepare the next step.

You might want to avoid the "narrator"- or "orator-type" styles that were designed especially for speeches. Although most books on effective speaking recommend these styles, too many of the letters look alike—particularly if you were to have the text typed out in all uppercase letters.

```
MITIGATE
WILLINGLY
FACILITATE
COMMITTEE
CRITICISM
```

Then, select a sans-serif typeface—one that lacks the little nubs on the bottoms and tops of certain letters. It is easier to read when you deliver your presentation. Notice the difference between the word "manuscript" in sans-serif and "manuscript" in a serif typeface.

Use upper- and lowercase letters. They will be far more readable when you take the next step.

If your equipment allows you to set the lines one-and-a-half spaces apart, use that setting. Single-spacing looks too crammed, and double-spacing is too wide for our purposes. Lines set one-and-a-half spaces apart make it easier for you to keep your place as you glance from the text to the audience and back.

Set your page lengths within the computer to print out no more than 15 lines of type, and do not split paragraphs or sentences from one page to the next.

Keep one point to a "page," and print each one on its own sheet. This will make it much easier for you to add, delete, or change your content at will.

As you move through this process, you may feel that you are devoting more time than you would if you just sat down and wrote a speech, made some changes, and delivered it. You're right: As with anything new, it will take you longer the first few times because some of that time is spent learning the process.

However, the time spent is an investment in the future, and each step in the preparation helps you to become more familiar with your material. This will help you ensure that the speech you deliver will achieve your objective.

Once you know the system, you will actually save time. Best of all, you will be developing presentations that will help you enhance your reputation. Do you recall the old saying: "Why is there never enough time to do the job right, but plenty of time to do it over?" Well, with careers at stake, why take chances?

"Eye-Cue™" Speech Preparation

The words in a speech text should never stretch from left to right across the page. Neat right-hand margins may earn compliments for typists, but they do little for presenters' delivery.

Even if you have learned to work with this "convention" and are willing to give neatness a higher priority than your own personal convenience—and effectiveness—you should consider the pitfalls. A poor line or page break can cause you to lose your place or concentration.

At a national conference a while back, a speaker read from a script he had obviously not rehearsed. He stumbled slightly through unfamiliar phrases, but the cruncher came at the end of the page where the secretary had incorrectly hyphenated a word to fill the line. The result was a page jump that read something like this:

"This is a great occasion for everyone. Each one of you can be proud of your personal contribution toward this, our largest condom-
_____ (page break) _
inium ever."

Experiences, such as this, can turn speakers into squeakers in a hurry, and this man was no exception. We'll speculate that he recovered his volume when he got back to the office and dealt with the typist. Of course, it was his error, too, for not rehearsing. But you know what we can do with that knowledge!

Here's the point: Always put complete thoughts on the same page. Never break a paragraph from one page to another. Thoughts that string through a line, jump from one line to another, and bump into one another can confuse, frustrate, and lead to insecurity, impatience, and worse. This technique will enable the presenter to keep his or her place, find the next phrase more easily, and, thus, deliver the talk with more confidence and expression.

Do all you can to help yourself. Stop the ideas from ramming, jumping, and bumping into one another. Your reward may be a smoother, more comfortable delivery that helps you build your confidence with each new speech you are asked to deliver.

The technique is simple. Prepare the speech in the traditional manner. Scan each line for places where either the thought breaks or you might be inclined to pause. Put double slashes (//) between the words where the thought breaks, single slashes (/) between the words, phrases, or sentences where you might pause. Wherever slashes suggest a break, move the information that follows to its own line. Continue this throughout the text.

Go back through each line, and weigh its contribution to the sentence or paragraph against whatever precedes and follows it. Decide whether each given line (using the reformatted text) is important enough to begin at the left margin, or whether it should be indented. Reformat each line accordingly.

Review what you have, deciding whether you can manipulate the text further to help yourself catch each phrase more easily as you glance back at the paper. For example, when you have a series of items of equal value or kind, run them as a list, one beneath the other.

When one phrase is clearly subordinate to another subordinate phrase, indent it further, much as you would an outline. When a phrase is too long for a line, find a logical break where you can shift it to the next line, indented.

An Example

The day Terry Anderson was taken hostage in Beirut, his good friend, Don Mell, former AP photographer, was on the scene. Here's how I helped Don tell the story by recasting the lines and doing some minor editing. This will illustrate the second paragraph:

ORIGINAL:

The morning started like any other 'normal' morning in Beirut. It was beautiful, sunny, crisp, and uneventful. Terry and I had just finished a game of tennis. He liked to play tennis to relax. He had things on his mind those days. He and his wife were expecting a new baby. He was worried about his dad's health.

FIRST PASS:

The morning started like any other 'normal' morning in Beirut.//
It was beautiful,/ sunny,/ crisp,/ and uneventful.// Terry and I had just

finished a game of tennis.// He liked to play tennis to relax.// He had things on his mind those days.// He and his wife were expecting a new baby.// He was worried about his dad's health.

SECOND PASS:

The morning started like any other 'normal' morning in Beirut.//
It was beautiful,/ sunny,/ crisp,/ and uneventful.//
Terry and I had just finished a game of tennis.//
He liked to play tennis to relax.//
He had things on his mind those days.//
He and his wife were expecting a new baby.//
He was worried about his dad's health.

THIRD PASS:

The morning started like any other 'normal' morning in Beirut. //
It was beautiful,/
    sunny,/
    crisp,/
    and uneventful.//
Terry and I had just finished a game of tennis.//
He liked to play tennis to relax.//
He had things on his mind those days.//
He and his wife were expecting a new baby.//
He was worried about his dad's health.

FINAL:

The morning started like any other 'normal' morning in Beirut.
It was beautiful,
    sunny,
    crisp,
    and uneventful.
Terry and I had just finished a game of tennis.
He liked to play tennis to relax.
He had things on his mind those days.
He and his wife were expecting a new baby.
He was worried about his dad's health.

Now let's apply the technique to a more-difficult paragraph from the same text:

Original:

I wanted to rescue Terry, but I couldn't. I wanted to run, but I couldn't do that. I just stood there in front of my home on a street so familiar to me, staring at a black pistol pointed at me by a man in his early twenties—a man my age. Not a word was spoken. At that moment Terry's eyes met mine. They said "Do something." Mine said, "I can't." Terry had the look of a man who knew he was doomed.

First Pass:

I wanted to rescue Terry,/ but I couldn't.// I wanted to run,/ but I couldn't do that.// I just stood there in front of my home on a street so familiar to me,/ staring at a black pistol pointed at me by a man in his early twenties//—a man my age. Not a word was spoken.// At that moment Terry's eyes met mine.// They said "Do something."// Mine said, "I can't."// Terry had the look of a man who knew he was doomed.

Second Pass:

I wanted to rescue Terry,/ but I couldn't.//
I wanted to run,/ but I couldn't do that.//
I just stood there in front of my home on a street so familiar to me,/
    staring at a black pistol pointed at me* by
        a man in his early twenties//
—a man my age.//
Not a word was spoken.//
At that moment Terry's eyes met mine.//
They said "Do something."//
Mine said, "I can't."//
Terry had the look of a man who knew he was doomed.

Third Pass:

I wanted to rescue Terry—but I couldn't.//
I wanted to run—but I couldn't do that.//
I just stood there in front of my home
    on a street so familiar to me,/
    staring at a black pistol (aimed) at me by
        a man in his early twenties//
        —a man my age.//

*I broke this line because it was too long, but left the word "by" at the end, so that the speaker would know he needed to carry the thought over to the next line.

Not a word was spoken.//
At that moment Terry's eyes met mine.//
They said "Do something."//
Mine said, "I can't."//
Terry had the look of a man who knew he was doomed.

FINAL PASS:

I wanted to rescue Terry—but I couldn't.
I wanted to run—but I couldn't do that.
I just stood there in front of my home
    on a street so familiar to me,
    staring at a black pistol (aimed) at me by
        a man in his early twenties—
            a man my age.
**There was silence.
Terry's eyes met mine.
They had the look of a man who
    knew he was doomed.
"Do something," they pleaded.
Mine said, "I can't."

That's the entire technique. It is flexible enough, so that once you have made all the obvious breaks and indentations, you can still modify the phrasings a bit more here and there. When you're done, you will have produced a speech that will be easy to present; one that will help build your confidence every time you glance at the script.

Printing Out Your Script

You are now ready to print your speech out in its final form. When you do, run two copies of it through a photocopier, enlarging the type about 15 to 20 percent—assuming that your printer uses either 10-point type or 12-point type. This provides better spacing between the words, lines, and paragraphs, and will help you find your place in the printed text more readily each time you look down—no matter how good your eyesight might be.

**Although I was asked to leave the script intact and concentrate on preparing the speaker and on recasting the speech only where it would aid delivery, I did shift the thought sequence and change the wording slightly here to give the words more impact.

You will use one copy for rehearsal, marking voice dynamics according to the system you are about to learn. The other copy will be the text you use for your presentation.

Most people are accustomed to having their speeches typed on standard, 8½- × 11-inch paper. This has its drawbacks, although legal-sized sheets are even worse. Manuscript pages tend to curl over, fall down, or slip off the lectern. I prefer 5- × 8-inch cards.

If you insist on using paper, do not staple the pages together or fold them. Instead, anchor them down at the lectern, so that they won't blow off when you gesture, or when the air-conditioning blower comes on.

As an added precaution, turn your pages sideways and print out your material only on the top half of each page. This has two benefits: Your pages are less likely to fall off the lectern, and it puts your words high enough on the page, so that you can keep your face toward the audience more often, instead of looking farther and farther down each page for your next lines.

By contrast, cards offer several advantages over sheets of paper: They are easy to handle. They are small enough, so that you can even carry the "deck" with you as you walk to your audiovisual equipment or toward the audience. (By the way, audiences don't mind you having notes at the lectern, and they won't mind seeing you carry them with you as long as you don't call undue attention to them.) Cards also have other advantages: They don't wrinkle as easily as paper; they can be held together with a rubber band instead of staples; and they fit into most jacket pockets or purses without folding. If your notes are too low on the lectern for you to maintain good eye contact, consider making a temporary ledge for them. (Again, cards have the advantage because they are sturdier.)

A Color-Code System That Gets You to Your Goal

When you prepare your final script, think of your end, middle, and beginning as a traffic-light system. Red equates with ending, yellow with middle (get ready to stop or proceed with caution), and green with beginning. If your printer will accept index cards, print out the appropriate parts of your talk on the cards. If not, you can always photocopy the material onto the color-coded cards later.

Should you elect to print your speech on paper (despite all my admonitions), you can still use a variation of the "traffic-light" system for color coding. You can print each part on paper of the appropriate color, or, if you only have white paper, you can draw a band of the corresponding color down the left margin of each page. If you are reluctant to do that for some reason, you can draw a yellow line at the bottom of your last "beginning" note to signal that the middle is coming next, and a red line between your middle and your ending to let you know you're about to enter the home stretch.

11
Delivering Your Presentation

You are now ready to prepare the rehearsal copy of your text for dynamic delivery. It may seem a little mechanical at first, but the technique enables you to decide—before you face the audience—what you want to emphasize, and how you want to deliver your message.

In an earlier chapter, we discussed the use of speech mark-up signals to help you deliver your talk with the proper dynamics, including tone, volume, pauses, and inflection. Now is the time to use them.

When you face an audience, you owe them more than to be just a talking head. You must convey your feelings—your enthusiasm, your energy, your emotions. If you give audiences less than that, you short-change them. You might just as well package your text, mail it to them, and save them the trouble of coming to hear and see you in the first place.

Audiences expect more than a mere reading of a script. It is a mistake to try to give "speeches" in this generation. We are used to receiving messages from people who speak to us in our living rooms, family rooms, and bedrooms—on television. Television is an intimate medium—people on TV don't have to "project." They talk in conversational tones, the way Donahue talks with them every morning—over coffee.

Because television has established the standards for communication in today's society and is a medium for direct involvement, it dictates the approach you must take with your audiences when you speak. People expect you to project the same kinds of feelings and emotions that they experience on television screens just ten feet from them.

To succeed, you must let audiences know how you *feel* and how you want *them* to feel. If Howard Beale in the movie "Network" had withheld his emotions and said, "I'm—ah—I'm mad as hell and—um—I—I'm not going to take it . . . any more," the line would have died.

When you try to read speeches, that's how you could come across. In today's society, it just doesn't work. People expect you to be in touch with your convictions and beliefs, and to express them through your voice and your gestures—not just through your words.

Conveying Your Convictions

You can get emotions across to any audience, in any situation. You can let them know what you're hoping to accomplish, what you would like them to believe as a result of hearing you.

In your talk, you can use your emotions to add impact as you raise new points. If you say, "Let's take a *look* at this!" you will have said something different from, "Now, if you'll notice on the left side of your screen, we have a slide that depicts. . . ."

You can clarify by saying, "I can easily *understand* how, looking at that slide, you might have *thought* that. Let's put it back *on* again, and take *another* look."

By managing your voice, gestures, eye contact, and voice tones, and coupling that with your willingness to explore a participant's concern, you have expressed empathy. Your attitude reflects your concern, courtesy, caring, and cooperation.

Feelings enable you to communicate more effectively as a presenter. You can use them to advise or to reassure. You can even use them to challenge others' *ideas* (as long as you don't challenge the person or try to take him or her on). The emotion you should communicate is: "We're all in this together, and we're addressing the issues. We're finding fault with the problem, not with each other."

You can use this technique effectively whenever you find yourself headed toward a "debate" with anyone in your audience. For example, if you're facing a hostile questioner who tries to take you on, consider saying, "Well, let's take a look at this, Joe. . . ." Avoid, "Joe, you're crazy. You're all wet!" The latter will get you in trouble because the rest of the audience will empathize with Joe, not with you. When you attack the issue, instead of Joe, the rest of the audience will be with you, looking at the problem. Now you can explore possible areas of agreement, and then work your way through those few areas in which you may have disagreements—not personal disagreements, but *conceptual* ones.

As you do, you will find yourself expending far less emotional energy, conserving it for more positive, constructive uses. Best of all, your audience will tend to support you—even when they may not agree with your point.

Emotions are an important way to convey your beliefs, and audiences want to know that you stand behind your convictions. How else might you use your emotions to appeal to your audiences? You can warn or challenge them, you can build a case or draw analogies, you can inspire or encourage them. You can appeal to them, motivate them, arouse them, calm them, placate them.

There are many possibilities. And you need nothing more than your voice and your body language to put them across. Remember, 93 percent of the total message an audience receives comes from your voice and your non-verbal communication. A low-key, monotone approach won't work. You've got to be up, enthusiastic, and energetic if you want to convey your beliefs.

Disclosure as an Aid

Disclosing something personal about oneself can be a useful way to convey your beliefs and convictions to your audiences. It can enable others see your more "human" side, to say, "I trust you," and to show listeners that in turn they can trust you.

In some ways, disclosure violates the "rule" that the person who listens holds more power than the person who tells. However, the level of risk depends largely on such matters as your ultimate motives and how much you disclose about what subjects and to what degree.

For example, it would be one thing to divulge that at age three you "stole" pennies from the kitchen counter and buried them in the garden because a bank commercial said that money could "grow." It would be quite different to confess that you once stole $50 from an open cash register in a neighborhood store. An even-higher level of disclosure would be to admit that you robbed a bank.

Self-disclosure carries another risk: It can turn into an exercise in *self-indulgence.* People who disclose may find themselves gaining so much relief that they lose sight of their original, valid intent—to encourage others to reveal more of their own feelings and thoughts.

How can you tell when you have disclosed enough, or whether you have gone too far? Here's a tip that can help: If you catch yourself speaking for a long time and hear yourself saying "I" or "me," use this as a signal to stop disclosing. Think of it as though you started to run some water in a sink, and it began to approach the brim. If you catch it soon enough, you can turn off the faucet or pull the plug (i.e., stop talking by giving the other person a chance to speak). If you don't catch it soon enough, you may find yourself having to "bail out" (i.e., get out of the entire situation as gracefully as possible).

When you give a presentation, and you find yourself "getting into deep water," you might try this "me > we > thee" technique: Stop talking about "me," and switch to a "we" approach that enjoins everyone to examine how "we all may have experienced something like. . . ." Then move right into a "thee" message, asking your audience to consider their *own* relevant experiences within the subject area. Finally, go back to the main point and summarize.

A DISCLOSURE DILEMMA

When you find yourself in a disclosure dilemma during an informal presentation, you can modify the technique this way: Switch from "me" to "you" by asking the audience members something, such as: "How do you feel about that?" Or, "Have you ever experienced anything, such as that?" Then, stop talking and listen. Encourage the person who responds by conveying friendly, interested eye contact and body language. You can also interpose an occasional, well-chosen word or two as long as your timing does not interrupt the individual's word flow or thought processes.

Appropriate self-disclosure can help encourage others to speak their mind and communicate their own convictions in what might otherwise be sensitive areas for them. When you use the technique, however, stay within the bounds of what you are willing to let become public knowledge, and be certain that you follow the rules outlined here.

Smile

Remember to smile when it is appropriate. A smile relaxes your face. It adds warmth and makes an audience feel more comfortable with you.

To get rid of a stern expression, overdo your smiling in practice sessions. During rehearsal, some speakers even draw big smile faces on easel pads and hang the sheets on chairs or on the wall in the back of the room.

A smile conveys friendliness, and friendliness is a feeling that doesn't come across often enough. But it can't be artificial. It must convey your true feelings and emotions. "I'm very happy to be here today," has to be felt to be convincing. Your goal is to win your audience, and this can best be done by getting your convictions across to them in a warm, sincere manner—with enthusiasm.

Putting Convictions in Writing

Once you are aware of the feelings and intentions you wish to convey in each part of your presentation, you can listen to yourself deliver it and mark your text to convey the dynamics you have had in mind.

Your next step, then, is to read your presentation aloud into a tape recorder. Make your points. Emphasize your words. Do exactly as you would if your audience were present.

Next, play back the tape and listen carefully to where you speeded up, slowed down, paused, tied phrases together, raised or lowered your pitch, or grew louder or softer. As you do, use the symbols presented on page 36 to mark your script lightly in pencil, according to the dynamics you feel are appropriate. As you rehearse further, feel free to change the markings to make your delivery even more effective. You may want to come up with additional symbols. Be creative. Develop whatever you feel will help you most.

Hundreds of participants in my workshops have listened to the following passage from this portion of John F. Kennedy's Inaugural Address (January 20, 1961):

> And so my fellow Americans:
> Ask not
> what your country can do for you—
> Ask what you can do
> for your country.

After hearing it, most have marked it up something like this:

And so / my fellow Americans: /
Ask not //
what your country / can do for you— //
Ask what you can do /
for your country. //

For practice on your own, look at the passage that follows. Read it aloud, then mark it to reflect the way you would deliver it. We have not offered you a "solution" this time. However you do it should be right for you. The test is to read it aloud into a tape recorder once you have marked it. Do this with any other material that will help you become familiar with this marking system.

> Everyone in this room is a professional communicator.
> You are. And you. And you.
> You say you are accountants—
> that you are not paid to write,
> speak,
> or edit.
> Yet every report that bears your name,
> every word you deliver at a staff meeting,
> every letter you write to a client,
> has a price tag.
> Industry leaders have said that
> given the choice between
> a whiz with numbers who can't communicate,
> and a mediocre numbers-cruncher who can,
> they'd hire the latter.
> Communication is the glue,
> the adhesive,
> the bonding agent that
> holds business together.
> Yes, indeed,
> every one of you in this room
> is a professional communicator.

At the Lectern

When you're finally ready to practice your technique at the lectern, there are two additional pieces of advice to know about, so that you don't have problems when you actually deliver your presentation. Don't get in the habit of "presetting" your notes, and don't flip your note cards over as you finish with each one.

Some presenters are sorely tempted to put their notes on the lectern well before they are introduced. Don't. I can't think of anything else a presenter might do that would so willfully put him or her in jeopardy with so little potential payout. Here's why: Often the person who introduces a speaker is more nervous and less well-prepared than you are. While thus distracted, he or she might pick up your notes—or part of them after introducing you. Presetting saves no time, and affords great risk. Simply put: Keep your notes with you at all times.

When you deliver a speech, do you generally work from pages and flip them over as you complete each one? If so, you have been creating an unnecessary distraction for your audience, taking the risk that you will snag one page with another and dump them on the floor.

Don't be a flipper; do be a slipper. If you put your first note to your left (or right) and the rest of the stack on the other side, you will have two from which to work—the one you are about to finish and the one you are going to need next. It does wonders to smooth one's delivery.

12
"Reading" Your Audience

When you speak, your audience will be giving you constant feedback from the moment you begin. I can recall giving one speech during which a fly kept circling around my face. Intent on what I was trying to convey to the audience, I ignored it. Had I been paying more attention to the audience members, however, I would have seen that the fly was distracting to *them*.

As the fly kept buzzing around my lectern and face, I finally realized that people were concentrating more on the fly than they were on my message. At that point, I rolled several sheets of paper from my handouts into a "fly swatter." As I did, I could see audience members smiling approvingly. When the fly landed, I dispatched it with one resounding smack. With that, someone spoke out with good humor: "We were wondering how long it would take before you did something about it."

That business out of the way, they paid closer attention. However, so did I—to my audiences' non-verbals—and have continued to do so ever since.

Audiences can tell you a lot, if you care to observe them. By their body language, they will let you know whether they are hot or cold, enthused or bored, supportive or in disagreement, and much more. They will let you know if you're running long, if you should call a break, and even if you have the wrong visual on a screen.

I once sat in on a presentation that particularly interested me at a national conference. The presenter had appropriately kept the lights on above the audience and off on the stage, so that the visuals would screen better.

Within a few seconds, this happened: He moved dynamically into his presentation, maintaining excellent eye contact with the audience. So intense was his focus on them that he failed to notice what was happening on the screen. Soon I concluded that he had his slides in the right sequence—but for a different presentation. The participants, polite to a fault, did not respond to the first few inappropriate slides. Then, as the problem became more evident, they began to fidget.

Four slides and 20 seconds into the presentation, the speaker happened to be telling the audience how to make one's talk a success just as a graphic illustration of an atomic bomb explosion flashed on the screen. I could tell that he was puzzled, but he moved on. The slide did not seem to match his words well, but the audience accepted what they saw and heard and settled back.

Three more slides, several seconds, and three more mismatches later, the audience began to fidget even more. Some tried making thrusting head motions toward the screen—to no avail. Their non-verbals were clear enough, but the speaker—still less than a minute into his presentation—continued without looking at the screen behind him. It was almost as though, by not looking, he could make the inevitable go away.

At a minute and counting, he said he would also be talking about sexism in language. Just then, he pushed the remote button, and an internationally known elder statesman popped onto the screen. The audience could no longer be controlled.

Wisely, the speaker apologized and called a brief recess. When we reassembled, he announced that he had, indeed, brought the wrong slide tray with him, apologized, and went on to deliver a fine presentation without slides. Ironically, though, every so often he would look back over his shoulder at the now blank screen. Perhaps once burned, he wasn't taking any chances.

Using Eye Contact to Build Support

Perhaps you've been told that good speakers always look at "the audience" when they talk before a group. Or, someone may have told you to "speak to the back of the room," or to speak to an audience member in each quadrant of the room.

If so, you may still not have found a satisfactory solution for making eye contact with your audiences. If you're still wondering what works, what doesn't, and why, here's some logic you might appreciate.

One of the values of making eye contact is to help break the invisible barrier between speakers and listeners. When speakers use eye contact effectively, it relaxes them, improves their presentation, and establishes a more conversational tone.

The key lies in selecting the right people with whom to establish eyeball communication. If you look at backs of rooms, you will receive no non-verbal feedback at all. On the other hand, if you just pick out people at random in various segments of the audience, you might pick the wrong ones. Yet, eye contact with individuals is important to your success. So, how should you pick them?

When you try this rapport technique, avoid people who are writing, reading, or otherwise engaged. If they're not looking at you, you will receive nothing from them for your efforts.

You should also avoid trying to engage people who have annoyed expressions (for whatever reasons), are falling asleep (for whatever reasons), or clearly disagree with you (again, for whatever reasons). None of these people will give you the non-verbal encouragement that effective eye contact can provide. When such people appear in your audience, don't take their attitudes, actions, or expressions personally. They rarely have anything to do with you or your presentation. To get the positive feedback that will help you deliver an even better presentation, select people who smile, nod their heads in agreement at appropriate times, display open body language, appear to be listening attentively, or show support in other ways, such as tapping a neighbor with a gesture that says, "I told you so."

"THE AURA EFFECT"

When you focus on various people who give you these signals throughout the audience, you are likely to mirror, or copy, their attitudes. By reflecting their positive feedback, you can radiate even more strength to your other audience members. Each time you look at a supportive audience member, your own positive body language and voice tones also receive another infusion of energy. Your eye contact with each one radiates to others around them.

I call this the "aura effect," and it is based on my extensive observations and follow-up over several years. I have found that audience members two or three rows in front of my "supporters," two or three rows behind them, and one to three people on either side of them said they felt I had established positive eye contact with them (although I had purposely not done so in tests). When you create the aura effect through effective eye contact with supportive members of the audience, you can reach out to even more participants and establish an even better rapport with them.

So when it comes to relating to audiences, the "eyes" have it. However, successful eye contact depends on whom you seek when you speak.

How to Lock In Audience Recall

There are several ways to boost your audience's ability to remember what you have said. The most obvious way is to repeat it. You may recall the old saying, "First you tell them what you're going to tell them. Then you tell them. Then you tell them what you told them."

Like most cliches, it must have value, or it would not have been around for so long. Repetition does, indeed, equate with reinforcement, so that what you repeat will be more likely to be recalled than what you say only once.

As improbable as it may seem, studies have shown that even repetition of bad news—say about a product—can result in positive benefits for the seller of that product. To recall another cliche that has survived, "I don't care what they say about me, as long as they get my name right." Time has a miraculous way of helping people forget bad news. Consequently, in cases such as this, only the name survives—often long after the bad news has been forgotten.

You can also enhance recall by having your audience respond to a certain message in a certain way, then coupling that message with some other signal, symbol, or words until they take on the same meaning as your original words.

Symbols have long been used to rally people instantly to causes just as effectively as people may have rallied when they heard the first speech on the same subject. The Statue of Liberty started out as a pile of metal, but today it is a symbol of freedom because that is the meaning that was assigned to it.

Symbols as tools for enhancing recall abound in our society. Advertising is filled with symbols and slogans that motivate those who see and hear them to take specific actions. I've never cared much for beer, but I still recall the jingle, "What'll you have? Pabst Blue Ribbon," although that commercial hasn't been aired in decades, and I have never tried the beer. It may not have motivated me to act, but it certainly enhanced my recall of the product.

Using Embedments to Increase Recall

Of course, audiences will recall more information when you present it according to all the criteria for good presentations set forth in this book. Presenting the information they expect to hear, in terms that are comfortable to them, according to their needs, motivations, and interests; speaking in words that are familiar and comfortable to them; and using such devices as triads—all enhance recall.

Behaviorists know another highly effective technique for enhancing recall: They call it embedment. Embedded suggestions are thoughts or ideas within a communication that have meaning or impact beyond the apparent or intended message, itself. Using embedments to obtain agreement and recall can help to overcome resistance from even the most difficult questioners and also help them to remember your message.

Here is the basic concept in action:

Questioner: "Do you really think that embedments can help people remember information?"

Your response: "Well, Mary, I would have to wonder whether paying close attention to the concept of embedments would be a good idea because researchers identified the technique by studying successful communicators and codifying their techniques."

Your voice tones should accent certain words, such as "paying close attention," "good idea," and "successful communicators."

On the conscious level, you should sound as though you were expressing your own views in a speculative manner: "I wonder whether . . . would be. . . ." On an embedment level, however, the listener's subconscious hears: ". . . paying close attention to the concept of embedments (is) a good idea."

Some people may be able to resist that kind of suggestion, but even those who depend heavily on their communications skills in their professions will recall it later. Thus, if you are addressing skilled communicators who may not respond to embedments as well as others, you might alter your words by saying, "I wonder whether *not* paying close attention to this concept would be a good idea."

Or you could even say, "Perhaps one might wonder whether paying close attention to this concept would *not* be a good idea." The theory behind this is that negative words, such as "not," tend to obfuscate or conceal the embedment further.

Still, some people might not respond to the embedment. Thus, when you know the pressure will be on, you might try this variation: "Some people believe that it's *not* a good idea to *not* pay close attention to this concept." This is what might be called a "double-whammy."

Embedments aren't limited to words, alone. They can be made with pictures and even odors—by knowing which sensory stimuli can trigger which specific emotions. You can even cause tactile embedments by touching someone at a specific time as you elicit specific words or feelings from them, or by having them do this to themselves.

Embedments are a reality. They are being used, and people will continue to use them, to persuade, enhance recall, and do much more. Like so many other advanced techniques, they have neither positive nor negative value of themselves. It is up to those who use them to determine whether they will serve society constructively.

Practice, Practice, Practice

You'd think you were finished by now. Not so. As any professional presenter knows, you have just begun. Go back and reread Chapter Six on rehearsal. Follow everything it recommends, and then you still have one more step: If you have rehearsed with someone critiquing you, you need to practice some more on your own. If you have rehearsed on your own until now, you'll need further practice.

No one ever said that becoming a good presenter was going to be easy. Facing audiences skillfully, like anything else you might want to do in life, takes practice—perfect practice—and lots of it.

As you go through these final rehearsals, imagine your audience in front of you; project your slides; write on the easel pad; display your overheads (more on audiovisuals later). Whenever you change visuals, place a symbol on your notes to remind you that there you intend to show the audience members something.

Work through the process until you have every *point* almost memorized—not the words, themselves, but the major points and the important supporting ones. Total rote memorization comes across as mechanical. It puts pressure on you to recall every word, and, besides, no one else knows what your next words should be anyhow. Therefore, no one can judge what you "should have said." Also remember that content is only a fraction of the total message, so don't burden yourself with the unnecessary pressure of total memorization. Let your rehearsals become one more way to build your confidence.

13
Special Presentations

Although the "end to beginning" technique can be one of the most effective tools you will have available to you as a speaker, there are times when you may not want or be able to use it. Perhaps you have been asked to talk about a subject you know so well that you don't feel the need to structure a formal speech. Or, you may not have received enough advance notice to work through the process. This chapter will help you improve your skills in the special situations you are most likely to face.

The Nonscripted Talk

There may be times that you may not need or choose to actually write out a formal presentation or follow the end-to-beginning structure to the letter. However, once you have practiced that technique, you will find that even your most casual presentations emphasize one of the five kinds of endings, middles, and beginnings. If your talks have been effective, they have probably followed the "gazinta" (goes into) process in which certain types of beginnings go into certain middles best, and certain types of middles go into certain endings best.

No matter how loosely you structure your presentation—even if you allow time for discussion between your key points—you will find that you have been following an organizational game plan all along. The key is to analyze it and make it work even more effective for you.

First, consider the topics on which you have spoken—and are most likely to speak—without notes. Now, consider how you have generally concluded your presentations in the past. Identify the components in your ending, and note the type of ending you have used. Do the same with the middle, paying close attention to the approach you have taken each time. You may find a pattern (one of the five types of middles) there as well.

Now, do the same with your opening. How have you started off in the past? Have you been consistent? Most likely you will find a pattern there, too.

If you don't have enough experience with nonscripted presentations to help you make these judgments, you can still apply the process. Simply go through the audience checklist and then ask yourself these questions:

- What's my bottom line? What do I want to leave this audience with? What kind of ending is this? What points should it include?
- What is the best way to structure the points I want to discuss? Would a problem-solution/cause-effect approach get the job done? (Many nonscripted talks use this kind of middle.) Would another type be more effective? Will it lead me into my ending easily?
- How should I open? What should I say that will help to flow right into the middle, or discussion aspect, of my talk? What kind of beginning is this? What points do I need to cover in my opening?

There may also be occasions when you would have chosen to develop your presentation according to the "Organizing Words from End to Beginning©" method, but you don't have enough time to do so. Even when the lack of a script is not a matter of choice and comfort with your material, you can still structure an impromptu talk quickly, if you have enough time to ask yourself the above questions.

However, if there isn't even time to do that, here's a quick survival tactic that my clients have used successfully: Terry worked for a major employer in the area in which she was attending a dinner of a local civic organization. Without warning, the chairperson asked her to stand up and "give a few remarks" about her firm's petition to reroute a public road.

The issue had been controversial, and Terry was not exactly pleased at being put in this position. However, she accepted it as an opportunity,

---

> "It takes three weeks to prepare a good ad-lib speech."
> *Mark Twain*

and wisely bought a little time by asking the chairperson to take care of the balance of the organization's business and then come back to her.

Within five minutes, she had recognized the potential controversy and had decided to address what was likely to be the audience's main, unspoken question: "What's in it for me?" She pulled together three concluding points that addressed this (reduced traffic, better flow, and rerouting to avoid a blind stop sign) and had a value-and-meaning ending under control.

With three minutes left with which to do an outline, she decided to use the same three points to form her middle and to expand on each. She thus had a topical middle.

Now, with the clock still ticking, and the chairperson already starting to look her way, she asked herself: How do I get to these three points? What should I start with? Since everyone at the dinner knew the situation, she decided to go right into the subject in general terms (everyone's shared concern for the increased traffic throughout the community in the past few years) and move directly to her firm's specific proposal.

She spoke for only three minutes, but she had a positive impact. Afterward, a few participants told her that her presentation helped give them a new perspective. One or two others commended her for accepting the challenge and doing so well with it.

Again, the bottom-line approach had paid dividends.

And Now, Heeere's. . . .

If you are called on to introduce someone or to present or accept an award, you have a key role in terms of your need to identify with your audience members' hopes and aspirations. They are counting on you to say what they wish they could say, as well as to make the comments they would like to hear.

INTRODUCING OTHERS

Introducing a speaker is like introducing someone to friends of yours who have made a considerable effort to be there for the occasion. Both your audience members and your speaker deserve the best you can give them and count on you to give each of them enough information to go on, so that their subsequent relationship will be a good one.

It is all too easy to fall into the trap of reading speakers' résumés when you introduce them. Generally, this takes too much time and covers too much irrelevant information. It also doesn't take into account the value you gain in cementing the relationship between speaker and audience by "introducing" the audience members to the speaker. Before you take the last phrase too literally, here's what we mean: Simply include information about why these people have gathered to hear this speaker. For example, does the organization gather each year to honor certain members for special contributions to the cause? No matter what the occasion, spell it out briefly, and then tell why you have invited this speaker for this purpose. Keep the introductory material brief and relevant.

If previous employers, academic degrees, and the like have no bearing on why you invited this person to speak, don't mention them. If they add significance to the occasion, but still do not fit into your introduction, include them in a longer biography that might be printed in your program.

Generally, your introduction should answer these questions: Why this person? Why this subject? Why this audience? Why here? Why now?

PRESENTING AWARDS

When you present an award, your words must speak for your entire audience because the award reflects their goals, objectives, and, often, ideals. You can address many of the same questions when you present the award, but then the perspective differs. You are not introducing the individual to your audience members. You are giving something to him or her on their behalf—something that represents their desire to acknowledge someone who reflects their own, or their organization's, highest aspirations.

Even if you are presenting "only" a plaque and a gold watch at someone's retirement dinner, you have the same responsibility as if you were presenting a special award to an Olympic medal winner. Ensure that your words speak to the goals and ideals that the award embodies. Tell something about this individual's achievement, and remind everyone of how he or she reflects those values. Then, allow your words to help the audience members share in the act of presenting the award.

Staging

Introducing a speaker or presenting or receiving an award can result in awkward moments for the unprepared. When you introduce someone or present an award, build your words carefully, and let both your words and your gestures show, clearly, when you are almost through and are ready to ask the speaker or honoree to come forward. This eliminates "false starts" that can be uncomfortable for everyone.

One executive told me about one occasion when the audience actually began to laugh. The person handling the introduction said, "It's a pleasure for me to introduce Mr. Smith." Taking this as his cue, Mr. Smith began to rise, only to hear the speaker say, "But before I ask him to come up here, there's something else you should know," and went on speaking. She repeated almost the same words, and again Mr. Smith started to rise, only to hear the same thing.

When this happened for the third time, he decided not to stand up—in case he was "wrong" again. This time, however, she stopped speaking. Through the thickening silence, she resorted to gesturing to him with both hands to come forward as the audience began to chuckle.

He vowed: "Never again!" Now, as all frequent speakers should, he writes his own introduction, types it in the Eye-Cue™ delivery format, and sends a copy to the person who will introduce him. (He even brings a spare copy with him.) He arranges to meet "the introducer" just before he goes on, and asks whether he or she has any questions. Most introducers appreciate this courtesy, and he is no longer caught by surprise when he is introduced.

As the introducer, it becomes your job to handle the podium "traffic." Will the presenter come up from your left or your right? Do you plan to shake his or her hand? Have you decided how you will leave the podium, and are you prepared to guide the speaker toward the lectern, so that he or she will know whether to pass in front of you or behind you?

Note: Once your speaker is on stage, you always take the background position. You "steer" the speaker in front of you, and then walk behind him or her when leaving.

If you are presenting an award, the same issues apply. However, you have another piece of "business" (to use a theater term) to transact before you leave: You need to present the award.

High school graduations always come to mind when I think about this process. The graduate comes forward, appearing uncertain whether to take the diploma and run, or do whatever else the pumping adrenalin sends his or her way. The internal dialogue is probably going something like this: "I hope I don't trip going up these steps. Wouldn't that look stupid! Do I reach for the degree with my right hand? If so, what will I do if the presenter tries to shake hands with me? After all, not everyone else shook hands. Oh no, Mom said she wants to take pictures. If I go up from my left and shake with my right hand, I'll be turned backward. Oh no, I'm there already. (BLANK) Good grief. I'm back in my seat. What happened? Well, it's almost over."

Help your award recipient. Go over the details ahead of time then stick with your game plan. Bring the recipient up from your right, if possible. As he or she comes up, hold the award in your left hand, or leave it where you can reach it easily without turning your back to the audience. Back away from the lectern or microphone, if you are using one, and immediately look at the individual's right hand as you reach out with your own right hand to shake hands. Next, smile and shake hands. As you do, you may need to use a little tugging pressure to "steer" the person to continue facing the audience. Now, break off the handshake, and pick up the award with your left hand (if you were not already holding it in your left hand), and place it in front of him or her, so that eye contact with the audience remains unbroken. Look at the award; look at the individual; and then leave as unobtrusively as possible.

Accepting Awards

This is not the time to do a Marlon Brando routine. The audience deserves more than a substitute, mumbled thanks, or a hasty walk off. You don't need to rattle on forever, but you should "share" this moment with those who made it possible.

Avoid the "Aw shucks" and "golly gee" routine. It serves no useful purpose and often leaves people cold. Again, they deserve and expect more from you. A gracious award recipient need not be especially eloquent to win the audience's hearts.

Years ago, when I was working in public relations for a utility company, I heard a "thank you" that I will never forget. It was spoken by a man who had never finished high school, had served our country at war for three years, and was just completing a career of 40-plus years with this same employer.

He said, in the best way he knew how, "I've 'clumb' many a pole in my lifetime—and so have a lot of you right here tonight. One day, many of you will be in the same spot where I'm standing right now. It's been many a year since I started with the company, and no watch or certificate in the world can ever take the place of what I feel right now. You're my friends, and I'd like to think that I've been yours. So when I hang this piece of paper on my wall, and when I look to see what time it is, I'll think about you—and the company that made it all possible. I'm going to miss you."

It may not have won any Oscars, but this was a warm, genuine thank you that took into account the audience's deepest feelings. I was not surprised to see a tear or two in more than a few eyes at that moment.

You Are in Charge

Finally, remember whether you are an introducer, a presenter, or a receiver, you need to know how to carry out your role, so that the greater purpose—addressing the audience's needs—is served best.

14
Special and Difficult Situations

No matter how well you prepare, you are bound to run into a "gotcha" situation once in a while. It happens even to those who speak and coach others for a living. I have had microphones go dead, entire portable screens fall over, an "aide" throw a two-projector presentation out of synch.

Once, I reached across the head table, which was on a dais, to shake hands with people at floor level and bathed my necktie in a glass of champagne. It had been placed there for a toast to the new president of a national organization to whom I was to bring greetings. To compound the embarrassment, when I went to draw back my hand and sit down, I tipped the near edge of the glass and dumped the rest of the contents into my lap. Fortunately, there had only been about an ounce of champagne in the glass.

It was a replay of one of Murphy's laws: If anything can go wrong, it will do so when you face an audience, and when the largest possible number of people are watching. How to deal with it? By staying calm and remembering that by the grace of God, this, too, will pass.

In this case, I simply used my napkin to blot up the wine as well and as discretely as I could, and gave thanks that the wet spot was low enough to be concealed by the table if it had not dried when it was time for me to stand and speak.

Dealing with Interruptions

Notwithstanding such accidents, interruptions are perhaps the most difficult problem for most presenters. With planning, most other situations can be anticipated and forestalled.

When you are interrupted, there is a good chance that the audience will also be distracted. They lose their concentration, you are thrown off stride, and an otherwise effective talk can be ruined—unless you anticipate even what can't be anticipated.

Ironically, staff people—either yours or the staff of the facility where you may be speaking—cause the worst interruptions. In off-site presentations, clients tell me they have had workers enter the room and even walk on or behind the speaker's lectern—sometimes carrying ladders, wiring, and other paraphernalia.

You can head off most interrupters by making certain that you have someone ready to take charge. I call this person my "gatekeeper." Meet with them ahead of time, and gain their commitment to keeping your room free of distractions while you are "on stage."

If a meal will be served before you speak, the gatekeeper's first job is to tell the person in charge of food services that all clearing should be finished before you start. They should stress that there would be strong things said about any food worker who even enters the room while you're speaking. They should do the same with any other person or the head of any other department that is likely to want access to the room.

If you have requested something, such as an easel, and it hasn't arrived before you start, tell your gatekeeper what you would like him or her to do if it arrives while you are speaking.

During one speaking engagement several years ago, I requested hot tea with the luncheon. It arrived 20 minutes later—waiter, pot, and all—at the lectern, on a raised dais, before several hundred people. As I began to make my most important point, the waiter jumped me from behind and said, "Still want this tea?" I managed to smile and say, "Thank you" (although I had other comments in mind), and continued speaking. However, I also vowed that it would never happen to me again.

Sometimes, difficulties occur because of something the facility's staff people have done, or allowed to happen, elsewhere. I have heard steam generators click on one wall away and rock bands start up on the other side of a partition. Perhaps one of the most stressful interruptions for me occurred when I was speaking in a rotunda, and water fountains began cascading behind me after I had begun talking. They were not overly noisy, but I am one of the many people for whom running water has a tremendous power of suggestion.

Whatever happens, if you have a gatekeeper, give a prearranged signal. No gatekeeper? Excuse yourself, and have the nearest available person take care of the problem for you. Usually a brief and courteous request made to the right person will expedite matters. On the other hand, if you have a problem in your room that needs to be dealt with— such as a defective pull-down screen—and you have requested assistance, you have two courses of action when the workers arrive: If the work will be done briefly, excuse yourself to the audience and pause. If it will take longer, call a short break. Naturally, this assumes that you still want the work done. If not, thank the repair person, and go on with your speech.

The same rules hold for photographers. If allowing them to take pictures will benefit you or your organization, permit two or three shots—even with a flash. Just be sure to look elsewhere. Then, immediately thank the photographer in a polite, but pointed, way that shows you expect him or her to stop right then. (Many presenters have shared enough stories about the "one-more-shot" photographer with me that I must emphasize this.)

Several books offer clever one-liners for dealing with people who interrupt presenters. The stories make good reading, and they probably did work for some speaker, somewhere, sometime. However, most of these ad-libs occurred spontaneously to accomplished, poised speakers.

Less-seasoned speakers may find that, in the stress of the distraction, they either miss the humor or sound sarcastic. Under stress, even the simplest "just-in-case" lines can fail.

Unless you can smile both inwardly and outwardly in the face of near disaster, you might not want to attempt a quip. Even so fundamental a rejoinder as "I see we have a volunteer already" could pose problems if the gestures and voice tones are not exactly right.

If the interruption is brief and not too distracting, ignore it. If it lasts longer and is more distracting, pause until it clears. If it is intolerable, stop.

To be more specific:

- If *one* person, at *one* table, gets up and leaves, ignore the interruption.
- If one table *full of people* gets up and leaves, pause.
- If *everyone* gets up and leaves, stop.

Keeping Old Talks Fresh

Here is yet another problem that poses difficulties of a different kind: I call it "keeping the bloom on the rose." If you have to give the same presentation repeatedly, you can quickly wilt from boredom. Your voice will be flat, low, and sluggish, and the audience will spot it at once. They'll conclude that since you are bored with what's going on, they should be too.

To keep a talk fresh, find a new way to end—even if you have to adhere to the same type of ending and can only juggle the elements. Consider new ways to shift the content of your middle without altering the meaning. Look for new "sparklers," and replace the old ones from time to time. If your routine has you presenting at the same time of day or on the same days of the week, come up with a fresh schedule. If you have been delivering your entire talk and only taking questions at the end, break your presentation into parts, and take questions at the end of each part.

If you really hit a saturation point, and you must go on, do a quick rehearsal, and play with the words. See how many ways you can deliver the most boring sentences. Suppose this sentence, for example, were included in your presentation: "Our department is always ready to assist you." You might see how many different ways you could get the same point across—either by changing the words or by the way you emphasize them.

Sounding bored is not the only risk. When you have to deliver the same talk too often, you may also tend to sound terse or sharp. Although you may have become annoyed with the talk or the situation, you don't want the audience to think these emotions are directed at them. You will have to work extra hard to remind yourself that, for them, your talk is new. Strive to keep your voice tones pleasant.

If you try to get your presentations over with by speaking too fast, the audience may think you're anxious or nervous. When you find yourself rushing, slow down. For your own "entertainment," vary your pace.

Another frequent result of speakers' boredom with having to repeat presentations is choppy sentences and long gaps. Nonwords, such as "um" and "ah," also tend to creep in. Try to overcome the tendency to use them by paying close attention to your meaning and by pacing your voice evenly.

Make certain your face reflects the kinds of feelings your voice is trying to convey. When the impressions people form by what they see conflict with what they hear, their subconscious often causes them to draw intellectual and emotional conclusions that may not be in your best interest.

Think about what would happen if you put on a bored expression and said to someone, "I love your new hairdo." No matter how convincingly you spoke the words, the visual impression would prevail. In our society, visual messages have more impact than auditory ones. So your facial expressions and voice tones have to be congruent with your words if you want to be convincing.

15
The Question and Answer Period

Responding to questions after a talk can be the most effective way to get your points across to any audience. Audiences generally remember longest what they hear last, and they retain more of what they participate in developing, discussing, or exploring. When you encourage audience members to ask questions, you evoke a higher level of interest in what follows—your answers.

Questions can give you a chance to make new points or clarify others that the audience may have misunderstood. They can also enable you to emphasize or underscore your more significant points.

Taking questions also enables you to learn what interests the audience beyond what you have already told them. They may hit on a point that could spell the difference between a successful talk and one that just misses the mark. Invite and deal with even the most hostile questions within the room. This is better than having to deal with unspoken problems that might arise later. A Q&A period provides a real opportunity for two-way communication—feedback that is essential to successful communication.

Audience's Agenda

When you respond to any question, keep the audience's personal agenda in mind. They want to know how your point is relevant to them. Address their needs and interests in your answers, and you will increase their receptivity and understanding. They may be pondering such unspoken

127

questions as, "So what" or "Who cares." *Tell* them what, and *show* them why *they* should care.

In a Q&A period within one's own organization, perhaps 90 percent of the questions will be nonthreatening attempts at clarification or understanding. However, you should understand the key techniques a questioner might employ—however innocently—so that you can handle Q&A even better from now on.

Start by having the right attitude. Adopt the position that "we are all in this together." Assume that all questioners are friends unless you turn them against you. Try to find as many areas of agreement with questioners and audience members as possible.

When you accept questions, put yourself on an equal level with questioners; get on the same side of the fence; attack issues, not people. This approach can help avert disaster.

The stress you might feel when someone asks a tough question can be translated into three responses: Fight (and anger often plays right into the questioner's hand), fright (which may inspire some people to try to intimidate you even more), or flight (and if you try to walk out on a questioner, you'll lose).

Remember, no matter what questioners try to do, you are in charge of *you.* Keep your own pace, and stay patient and calm. Always try to help achieve understanding. Never turn up the heat.

Regardless of what you might have concluded from the Rather/Bush confrontation, unless you are ready for the presidency, don't try that tactic. When you become aroused or angry, interviewers and their audiences will wonder how you might handle more critical matters and how much of your message may be based on emotion rather than fact.

Use each question as an opportunity to show that you are a courteous, cooperative, and calm guest who is willing to share your knowledge of the subject. Maintain this attitude, and you can learn to enjoy handling questions successfully from any source.

How to Anticipate and Disarm Opposition

When you handle questions, you can sometimes experience pressure-filled, tense moments—particularly when facing questioners and audiences who hold opposing views. One way to deal with resistance or opposition is to ignore it. Most opposition will die of its own accord when left alone. When it doesn't, other factors may be involved, factors often determined by the personality of the questioner.

Without delving further into personality theory, here are some tips that will help you defuse most disagreement before it becomes an issue. These tips will enable you to anticipate and deal with problems before they arise.

Preface your presentation by noting that you are aware that all members of the audience may not share your views. Tell them that you appreciate their taking the time to listen and giving you the opportunity to share your views with them. Then, in your talk, begin with areas of mutual agreement to build as many common bonds as you can, while minimizing any differences you might anticipate.

Your opening might go like this: "I appreciate this opportunity to speak on the need to change our procedure for processing expense account vouchers. I know that each of you has expressed a view on this issue and that some of your views differ from what we plan to propose at this meeting. I am grateful for your willingness to listen, to hear all sides, and to contribute to the discussion. With your input, we'll be able to devise the best procedure possible. One thing I've found in our private conversations on this matter is that we do share many views. First, we agree that. . . ," (and so on).

You can also call for a show of hands from "opponents" on any tough issue for which you seek support, starting with an aspect about which you would anticipate the least resistance. You will either identify the extent of your opposition, so that you can deal with it, or you will discover what researchers have observed: Most people are reluctant to raise their hands when asked to show their support for the negative side of an issue. Thus, your next step should be to call for a show of hands from "supporters" on the positive side of the question. Then thank them, and proceed.

If you have laid the groundwork for support well before and during your presentation, but you still have aggressive questioners, stay calm. If they have an irrefutable point to make, let them make it. You don't have to agree with them, but you can say you appreciate their right to hold a different view, and thank them for sharing it with you. Doing this enhances your own credibility and the audience's empathy.

It bears repeating: Never debate questioners. That would provide them with a platform even larger than your audience would be willing to grant them. In your response to any opposition, bridge to the most positive point you can make, and direct your eye contact and body language in a friendly way toward someone who appears to be more supportive.

When possible, try to iron out potential differences well beforehand. If individuals are aggressive in talking with you before you speak, stay calm. When you handle questions later, if the same person makes a point that you can't refute, listen to it carefully. When necessary, you might have to say, "We have a different way of looking at this. . . ," and then go on to make your own point. However, if you can agree with the questioner's point (or at least with the issue behind it), do so. Then bridge to a positive point of your own.

When your information is solid, even those whose views may be contrary to your own are actually doing you a favor by challenging you: They are letting you know what they believe to be true and giving you the opportunity to be heard. They are also allowing you valuable time to share your views with others. Your responses should reflect this and should build on common bonds and shared ideas, while minimizing differences as much as possible.

During your responses, you might comment on any statements that agree with your view or indicate a common interest. These should be brief, such as: "Since we share this in common. . . ," or "I'm glad we agree on this issue. . . ." Then get on with your answer at once.

Try Understanding

First, sprinkle your presentation with statements that show "understanding." You might preface a remark by saying, "I understand how you feel about. . . ." Or, you might set up a situation that others are likely to bring up, and then say, "I might believe that, too, if that had been my experience." Or, you might say, "You have a *right* to think that, based on what you heard previously."

Throughout your talk, remain patient, and keep a calm demeanor. If you display any sign of irritation or annoyance—especially if your "critics" are sending out negative non-verbal signals—opposition is even more likely to erupt.

It might help to keep in mind that when people express opposition, they are really expressing their feelings—not attacking you. And, everyone is entitled to his or her own feelings. When you are convinced of that, you will be better able to deal with the opposition, just helping the other person change his or her feelings on the matter.

There are several ways to do this. You might consider these:

• You might reduce the intensity of the individual's emotions by asking him or her to tell you what would make them most uncomfortable. For example: Critic: "This plan can't possibly work. Why, I couldn't possibly do without three staff members for the next two weeks—no matter how important your deadline is." You: "I can appreciate your concern for your immediate priorities. Recognizing the problem we're all up against, what adjustments or accommodations would you be comfortable making?"

• You can also ask your critic to substitute one thought for another by changing the subject, by having audience members think about the same subject in a new way, and by talking about pleasant things. For example: Critic: "I can't possibly meet that deadline." You: "Think about it this way. Once you have this project out of the way, you can finally take your vacation."

• You can also convert negatives to positives. For example: Critic: "I don't care what the company's policy is. I'm not going to expect my people to work all these extra hours just to meet a deadline on this project." You: "Well, another way to look at is that some of them may welcome the overtime pay. Others may be just as happy as we are to get this project out the door."

Acknowledge resistance as soon as you become aware of it, even if you have to interrupt your presentation to do so. Let critics know you are aware of their previous positions, or address them when you believe you see negative signals in their non-verbals.

Learn to identify the differences between active and passive resistance. A passive resister may become silent or walk away. Such an individual may be avoidance-motivated, but his or her behavior makes a clear statement. It is best to leave them alone because to pursue the sensitive subject might cause them to react aggressively. An active resister, by contrast, has a repertoire of several verbal and non-verbal devices. In extreme cases they might even become physically violent. The resistance would still be active even though the resister might remain silent.

Here are some techniques from the behavioral sciences that can help you move through and beyond resistance:

• Future Pacing—"Once we finish our discussion, you might want to consider that point again."
• Embedment—"You might want to consider whether *your views have changed* once you have had a chance to read the report."

- Switch Subjects—A momentary shift of topics may reduce the resistance.
- Offer a Benefit—Show how compliance with your viewpoint will pay dividends for the listener.
- Draw Out Resistance—Get your critics to discuss every aspect of their opposition. Once the most outspoken individuals have talked themselves out, ask them whether that means their resistance is absolute.
- Compare Their Point with That of Others—The pain of a hangnail pales against that of a broken finger.

Reducing the Likelihood of Resistance

In all presentations, you can reduce the likelihood that resistance will arise just by establishing a comfortable environment. People resist more when they stand, less when they sit; more when they're tired, less when they're rested; more when they're under pressure, less when you take the pressure off.

When people have put innumerable stumbling blocks in your way, challenge their reasoning without appearing to threaten them or their position. Try to have them bring out the intensity of their resistance. One way to do this is to ask them directly if they oppose your ideas. For example, you might ask, "If I understand you correctly, you want to continue things the way they are, and you are not interested in knowing whether this proposal might be an improvement. Is that correct?" It's extremely difficult for any critic to maintain his or her opposition when you address them with a response this powerful.

You can also defuse opposition by dealing with the objectors before they attend your presentation. If possible, visit or call your known "negators" and "nay-sayers" before they become members of your audience. Tell them what you will be talking about, and give them a private opportunity to air their reactions. Then, in your presentation, you may be able to turn their negatives into your positives before issues become polarized. You will also have diluted any resistance that might have been forthcoming. It's difficult for anyone who was invited to contribute to the process beforehand to justify being critical of it later.

A healthy way to look at resistance is to know that whenever it occurs, it contains a benefit that just hasn't been explored. Thus, we can help ourselves by seeing the roles of others in a positive light, so that we can respond to them as constructively as possible.

Why Is There Resistance?

Why do people resist? Perhaps because they are afraid of ideas that differ from their own. They may distrust others' motives. They may lack personal convictions. They may want to avoid being told what to do. They may need to prove their strength. They may fear repercussions from their superiors.

Some may resist because they are in a bad mood or bad situation, because they don't want to give up "territory," or because they don't like the person making the proposal (and we can't please everyone). They may fear the unknown or like the status quo. Some may even believe they are being "set up" by the way you happened to open the presentation.

Finally, and let us not forget it, still others may simply have valid reasons for disagreeing. And, most important of all, some may even have better ideas!

I Agree, but. . . ."

"Yeah, but. . . ." This phrase may be one of the most frequently spoken, yet instantly devastating, responses in the English language.

When spoken, the phrase seems harmless enough. Most listeners don't even appear to notice the subtle messages of opposition and disagreement it contains. Yet, when you respond to any questioner with "but," the outcome is destructive even if you express it in such words as, "That may be right, but. . . ."

The root of the problem may be this: When trying to counter the objections of a difficult questioner, you may feel the need to try to "win." This may create resistance instead of rapport, and "Yeah, but . . ." can trigger the other party to respond defensively.

The implications of "Yeah, but . . ." can impact on the questioner's subconscious—even when he or she does not respond in words. Once that impression has been made, only a highly skilled communicator can keep it from gnawing away at all further communication—especially over time.

Remember, your goal is to create harmony, not discord. Try to find ways for your response to blend in with the other person's statements. Instead of countering with a "but," try an "and" approach. Here are a few to consider:

- If you can agree with the speaker's views, say, "I agree with you, *and.* . . ." Then continue on with your own views.
- If you cannot agree with the speaker's statement, try saying, "I can understand how you might believe that, *and.* . . ."
- If you're not comfortable going even that far, there's still another alternative (particularly when the other party's emotions are strong). Try saying, "I can respect your feelings, *and.* . . ."
- You could also maintain rapport by saying, "I appreciate your desire to [get some action on this issue, get these people moving, find a solution, or whatever the speaker hopes to attain], *and.* . . ."

The word "and" removes the opposition implied by "but" and communicates a desire to be agreeable. That, in turn, helps prepare the questioner to be more receptive to your offer of another way to consider the matter. It also allows you to speak to the issue, without attacking the "rightness" of others' viewpoints.

The technique takes practice, and as you face each urge to say, "Yeah, but. . . ," remember that you don't have to respond with a statement at all. When the issue, the individual, or the situation is particularly sensitive, here's an alternative:

Find something from the other person's end of the conversation that might bring the two of you into closer agreement, and ask a question about that. Avoid questions that can be answered with a short "yes" or "no." Remember, too, that questions that begin with "how" are better received than those that begin with "why," especially in tense situations. "Why" questions sometimes sound confrontational.

If you don't feel that even this approach will work, don't despair. Try allowing a pause of about ten seconds, possibly accompanied by a thoughtful "Hmmm" (you don't have to hum for the full ten seconds, of course), as you reflect on what you have heard. Stay calm as you wait. The key is to remain silent until the other person speaks again. Your patience will likely be rewarded with a clarification, or even a change of topic—not a bad outcome under the circumstances.

If you do try the silence method, and find yourself about to fill the verbal gap, say something that can't possibly arouse disagreement. For example, ask about the climate of the room. A typical question might be: "Is it too cool [smoky, warm, dim, etc.] in here, or is it me?" Then wait for the other person's response. It breaks up the pattern, and makes it less likely that he or she will pursue the topic. The least you'll gain is time to consider a better response.

If the individual persists in going back to the sensitive topic, consider whether he or she is being a boor or a bully, and whether you should continue the exchange at all. Some people may be verbally destructive in a given situation and may try to defeat you—or, sometimes, set themselves up to be defeated.

Extricate yourself as graciously as possible. Your exit line might range anywhere from, "Thank you for sharing your views with me. Let me take some others' questions now," to "You have obviously given your views some careful thought. My best bet is to accept that as fact." Then, looking elsewhere, say, "Next question, please."

There is yet another alternative if none of the approaches so far appears right for you, and you feel a "Yeah, but . . ." coming on, try a non-verbal response instead. Shift your posture in a major way. If you have your arms folded, uncross them. If you are leaning back, lean forward. Cough. Look around suddenly at some perceived distraction. If you are eating, wipe your mouth with your napkin, sip some water, or drop your fork. Generally, anything that interrupts the rhythm of a dialogue so obviously will bring about a change in topic, if not in attitude.

Some communications specialists call these techniques verbal and non-verbal redirects. I just call them plain good sense. They remind us of an important aspect of all communications: We can best succeed in relationships with others by first acting on what we can change about ourselves. If you feel yourself about to respond to that with a "Yeah, but. . . ," you might want to read this through one more time.

As you deal with difficult questioners, you may find it hard at times to control your own emotions. Perhaps you will be more successful at doing this if you remember something we touched on in an earlier chapter: You *can* take charge of your feelings. You don't have to feel any emotions that you choose not to feel. Nobody can make you feel angry, or irritated, or threatened, or argumentative, or hostile, or defensive. Nobody can *make* you feel anything. Your feelings are *your* choice, so avoid the tendency to react negatively toward the opposition you may encounter during a Q&A period. Look at the other side.

When you deal with difficult people, you have a responsibility to yourself to seek out and experience the positive feelings, the positive emotions, that are always present. Remember, the thorns are only one part of the rose bush: The blossoms are on top. Focus on the roses. They're there. For every negative, there is a positive. For every wrong, there's a right. For every down, there's an up. It's a law of nature.

Opening and Closing the Q&A Period

If you don't want to handle questions because of time limitations or other reasons, this technique will help you close an obligatory Q&A session quickly without appearing to be offensive: Pack up your speech note cards or your visual aids, *look at your watch,* and say, "I know we've covered a lot of ground here, and I don't suppose there are any questions (avoid eye contact), but I'd be willing to stay behind and speak with any of you who might have something they feel they *need* to pursue." Then immediately say, "Thank you again for your *time."* Look away from the audience, and leave the lectern, microphone, or any other symbol of "center stage."

If, on the other hand, you want to encourage questions, establish eye contact with the more friendly or supportive faces in your audience, smile, and say, "I'd be pleased to discuss (topic) with you more informally now. Who would like to start us off?" Some questioners may be as apprehensive about asking questions as you are about trying to answer them. It often takes courage for people to ask questions. Make it easy for them.

If hands don't go up right away, be patient. It can take as long as ten seconds before someone asks the first question. And, unless you have experienced this before, ten seconds can feel like a lifetime. Just be patient with your audience and yourself, and smile encouragingly.

If you still don't see a hand after ten seconds, raise your own hand, and say, "I'd be happy to take your questions now," with an approving nod. Often, someone will mirror your gesture and raise his or her own hand. If that doesn't elicit a response, call on someone who may have asked you a question before your talk, and ask them to *share* that with the others.

If that, too, doesn't get things going, ask yourself a question. Here's how: "The other day when I was visiting the regional office, someone there asked . . ." (repeat a question from that experience). Now answer that question briefly, and then turn to your audience, and say, "Who has the next question?"

If even that fails, you might try this: "I know how difficult it can be to ask the first question, so let's skip that one and go to the *second* question. Would someone like to ask *that* one?"

Only the most hardened audience would fail to respond to all these choices. If you still don't receive any questions after this much effort, repeat your strongest point briefly, thank your audience and your host, and walk off with the feeling that you have done your job well.

How to Conclude

When questions begin to repeat themselves, or when you sense a winding down, say that you have time for one or two more questions. If you like the first one, end on a high note. Otherwise, take a second question, and make the best point possible in your closing remarks.

16
Advanced Techniques for Handling Questions

People ask millions of questions of one another every day in this country. No subject is too sacred any longer, no topic too personal for inquiry. Television has set the standards for all forms of oral communication in today's society, and audiences are learning to emulate the skills of the professionals whom they see each day in their living rooms. Local and network news programming has expanded, and talk shows have proliferated.

As people learn to ask questions in more sophisticated ways, they bring new challenges to those who must respond in public forums, business meetings, and so on. The techniques are available for all to learn—on many different levels. Consequently, executives are finding it necessary to learn how to deal successfully with questioners' styles in their own audiences.

All of the techniques covered here are used by reporters on the air. No one technique is particularly clever once you understand it. Most of them are merely attempts to get at information, and reporters, in particular, use them when the speaker appears to be unprepared, uncooperative, unskilled, or boring. Some may be totally inappropriate for certain situations in which you may receive questions—but it is better to know about them and be overprepared than not know about them and be underprepared. You may never have to face reporters, but you may well face audience members who ask the same types of questions.

Some questions might cause you to want to speak off the record, or answer, "No comment," or repeat negative charges. These are particularly "loaded" situations—traps—and I always advise my clients to be careful not to take the bait.

Stay on the Record

Never speak "off the record" to anyone, regardless of how well you know the person. People tend to forget what was supposed to be kept confidential. In fact, some organizations have become skilled in their use of the "grapevine" for leaking information. I knew an executive who wanted to determine what his staff's reaction would be to moving an executive into another slot—before he risked announcing a shift. So he left a draft memo out on his secretary's desk, sent his secretary on an errand, and then invited an employee whom he knew to be a busybody to come to his office. He kept this individual waiting for several minutes near the secretary's desk as he sat behind closed doors.

The meeting was brief, and within hours the boss was receiving calls from several members of the staff who were eager to express their views on the "forthcoming move." When he heard the reactions, he decided to deny any part in it. This left the rumormonger, whose own credibility was not the greatest, to fend for himself, since he couldn't very well admit having snooped on the boss's secretary's desk.

"No-Comment" Answers

Never say, "No comment." People have come to regard it as an automatic self-indictment—a person who uses this response has something to hide. If you cannot comment on a question, say why, and either offer to get back to the person when things change (say, when a legal action is resolved, and your hands are no longer tied), or offer the questioner information of equal or better value. If, for instance, you can't provide a figure because of competitive reasons, you might say, "I wish I could share that information with you, (questioner's name), but that's a number that the head office is not releasing. But what I can tell you is this . . . ," and provide an industry figure or a number that you can discuss. Cap off your answer, of course, with a positive point.

When Asked Negative Questions

Never repeat a negative. Audiences tend to remember what is repeated or reinforced. If the questioner asks, "Do you disagree with the chairman?" do not answer by saying, "No, I don't disagree."

If you do that, your questioner and the audience hear "disagree" twice—prefaced by your "negator" words "no" and "don't." Since these negator words have minimal value, people's conscious minds tend to drop them. By contrast, negative words, such as "disagree," remain powerful.

Strange as it may sound, by the end of a week, people who hear "denial" statements may tend to believe that they recall hearing you say something negative about the chairman. They may know better, of course, but somehow that concept can get lodged in their subconscious. That says much about the power of negative words and why you should avoid them.

Use only positive words. Make only positive points. Convey only a positive attitude. This is the way to succeed.

When You Don't Know

If you don't know the answer to a question, say so, and offer to get the information back to the questioner. Your offer will enhance the audience's perception of you as courteous and cooperative. Be sure to follow through. This will boost your credibility. Once you've given your "don't-know" response, move on. It is better in this case to show wisdom through your silence than ignorance through your words.

Note: In any response, avoid negative words, technical jargon, or words and phrases that may be unfamiliar to the audience.

Types of Questions and How to Handle Them

If you are well-prepared to give interesting and informative responses to the questions you are asked, you have nothing to fear. Once you learn to recognize and understand the techniques, you will be able to respond to them unemotionally in the future.

Technique: Needling
Example: "Oh, come now. Do you really expect us to buy that?"
Response: Stick by your guns. Don't equivocate or vacillate. Say, "Absolutely, John." Then reinforce the positive point you've just made, or make a new positive point.
Technique: False Facts (unintentional or deliberate)
Example: "So you made a 72 percent profit last year?" (Actually it may

have been 11 percent, but up 72 percent from the comparable quarter last year.)

Response: Avoid the tendency to respond as though the facts were accurate. If you know the statement is wrong, correct it graciously: "Perhaps I could clarify that for you, Mary." Then go on to make a positive point about how the profits are used to provide jobs, invest in research, and so on. If you are unfamiliar with the information in question, acknowledge this, and say that you are, therefore, unable to comment on it. If the questioner persists, ask him or her to provide you with the source, so that you can report back afterward. This shuts off an unproductive line of questioning, keeps you out of a trap, and still shows cooperation.

Technique: Reinterpretation of Your Response

Example: "So what we have here is a possible failure?"

Response: Avoid repeating loaded words: (Pause) "Peter, what we're saying is that this segment of our business was not up to our expectations in the first quarter, and we are. . . ." Then go directly to what you're doing about it, and end on a positive point.

Technique: Putting Words in Your Mouth

Example: "So you're saying you think the procedure should be scrapped?"

Response: Recognize that to repeat these words is to add credence to them through verbal reinforcement—even if you are repeating them as part of a denial. Never use words you don't like, and don't argue with the questioner. Instead, say, "Let's see what's at issue here, Anne, if I may." Then make your positive point.

Technique: False Assumption or Conclusion

Example: "So, after you get these procedures in place, they'll shut down this location, right?"

Response: In your response, call the technique for what it is: "Well, Jim, that's an assumption I don't believe we should make." Or, "I don't think I could agree with your conclusion, Jim." Then go on to your positive point.

Technique: Hypothetical Question

Example: "If management reverses its long-standing position on. . . , our department will suffer, won't it?"

Response: Call the shot, but watch your voice tones: "That's a hypothetical question, Pat, and there are just too many unknowns here at the moment. What we hope will happen and are working toward is. . . ." Go on to make a positive point.

Technique: Baiting You into Accusations

Example: "What do you really think of (person/organization)?"

Response: When you wrestle with a pig, you both end up covered with mud. Don't play the game. Instead of demeaning the opposition, say, "Steve, if you talk with them directly, I feel you'd get a better answer on that. What I can tell you is this. . . ." Go on to describe your position on the issue, and end with a positive point.

Technique: Leading Question

Example: "Given your department's history of labor problems, how do you suppose you are going to deal with the union if you have more problems like the last one?"

Response: Don't be led into statements you do not choose to make. Let the questioner know you understand the technique by saying: "I'm not sure where you want to go with that [use the individual's name here to soften the impact], but. . . ." Then make almost any relevant point you prefer.

Technique: Multiple-part Question

Example: "How is the XYZ division doing? Is it going to be affected by the cutback? And if so, how much? Do you see an end in sight?"

Response: Pick the part you *want* to answer, and reply to that. You are under no obligation to try to respond to every part.

Technique: Forced-choice Question

Example: "Which is of more concern to your department, better productivity or your employees' complaints about working overtime?"

Response: Make your *own* selection. Choose either part, both parts, or neither of the choices the questioner offers you.

Dealing with Loaded Questions

The techniques that follow require more detailed discussion than other questions you might receive because they are more complex to understand and to handle successfully.

Technique: Loaded—False Statistics

Example: "Isn't it true that you exported over 1,000 jobs last year?"

Response: The trigger word is *exported*. When such loaded "statistical" questions come at you, go right to the nonweighted, non-emotional issue at the root of the question. When you do, "exporting jobs" becomes "hiring practices," and your answer might sound like this: "On the contrary, we, in fact, created 200 *new* jobs here because of the overseas expansion—an expansion that could not have occurred in this country, and one which brings direct income into this country to improve our balance of payments, I might add."

When a question hinges on a statistic you know to be inaccurate or false, question it. Ask the source. Ask the questioner to hold up the document the question is based on. Ask him or her to hand it to you. Remain courteous. If you know that the statement is not true, but you don't have the correct information in your hand, you would be unwise to try to refute it there and then. Instead, politely say that you don't believe that the information is correct, and leave yourself a way out, so that you can graciously offer to get back with a clarification or correction.

Technique: Loaded—Faulty Logic
Example 1:   "If nylon is so strong, why don't companies make indestructable nylon stockings?"
Response: A questioner who uses faulty logic makes factual leaps that overlook common sense. It could be worse: An individual once argued against daylight savings time because she said the additional hour of sunlight would burn up her grass. In the nylon-stockings example, comment on such problems as the thinness of the strands, the open weave that can catch and snag, and so on.
Example 2:   "Ever since we started operating the steam plant, people have been complaining that the fog in this area has been unbearable. How do I respond to them?"
Response: This accusation may totally ignore such facts as the presence of the same weather system even 20 miles away, or that the weather bureau has a perfectly logical atmospheric explanation for the fog that occurred the first three nights your plant happened to be in operation. When you point out facts such as these, your questioner will be able to accept them, unless he or she intended to be disagreeable.

To deal with faulty logic, you may also want to consider gaining audience support in a whimsical way—as long as you feel comfortable doing so. For example, you could point out other nonsensical corollaries, such as this: "That would be about as logical as saying that the local dog population has increased because the community installed fire hydrants."

Be careful not to insult your questioner, however. Stay in good humor by prefacing with, "I suppose we might also be able to conclude . . . ," or, "Following that kind of logic. . . ."

Stripping Loaded Questions

Loaded questions can cause you to feel set up to respond in ways that are inconsistent with how you would like to respond. Some people who ask loaded questions clearly intend to box you into tight corners. Others may do it innocently as part of their personal style. In either case, you have no obligation to allow a loaded question to "victimize" you, no matter who asks it.

Fighting back risks creating a "win-lose" situation that might inspire the "loser" to retaliate. You could try to "call the shots" by saying, "That's a loaded question." However, if you follow that with anything along the lines of ". . . and I'm not going to respond to it," you've again left yourself open to attack.

Here is a better approach—one that has worked hundreds of times, even in the most stressful situations. First, listen carefully to the question, pause, and isolate the loaded aspect. Then single out the loaded words. From there, determine the actual issue. Next, consider how you might neutralize the question. Finally, select a way to begin your response, so that you will show empathy and also buy a few seconds to think.

For example, suppose someone asks, "Do you think we are actually ripping off the public with our excessive overcharges?" Remain calm. Put your emotional energies into the intellectual game that faces you. Ask yourself the questions we've discussed:

What are the loaded words? "Ripping off," "excessive," and "overcharges."

What's at issue here? Prices.

How can I strip this down to a neutral question? Address the issue, not the words.

How can I begin with an empathetic statement that also gains time to put my thoughts in order? Start by acknowledging the individual's emotions, position, or view. Then begin with an opener such as one of these:

- "You evidently have strong feelings about this, Barbara."
- "I can respect your views on that, Barbara."
- "That may be your position, Barbara."

Then go on to say something such as this: ". . . and if I understand you correctly, the issue here is the prices we charge. On that issue, we can all be proud of our record. Our prices are consistent with the risks we take in bringing them to market, and our profit is actually lower than the industry average."

Then, without pause, give an example and conclude with a case that substantiates your statement.

You will have used fewer than 60 words, plus whatever additional words you need to give a brief example. Since 150 words per minute (or slightly more than two words per second) is an average speaking rate, you have used only 30 seconds. And since most questioners will not generally interrupt an answer that lasts 45 seconds or less, you still have time for another 30 words or so.

In less than a minute, you will have stripped the loaded question down to a neutral issue, said something positive about prices, and cited an interesting example. Your reply—consisting of both a positive attitude and positive words—will tend to lead follow-up questions into more constructive areas, or leave the matter where it stands.

Best of all, you will have shown your ability to stand up to this kind of pressure without making either party a "loser." This makes it difficult for the questioner to push the issue, and any attempts to go back to loaded questions or other manipulative methods will be seen for what they are.

The lesson is clear: Remain confident and in control of yourself and your responses, and you will gain everyone's respect—including your own.

At the risk of overstating the obvious, remember that you can turn each technique into a positive point. Regardless of the technique used, cooperate—don't compete with the questioner. Instead of anticipating a confrontation, approach every question as an opportunity. Talk with, not at, all questioners.

To Gain "Think" Time

When you need time to think about how to answer a complicated or complex question, there are responses you can use and some you should avoid. For example, don't say, "That's a good question," or, "That's a good point." These, along with, "I'm glad you asked that question," or, "I'm glad you brought that up," are obvious stalls for time—especially when there is clearly no reason to be "glad." Avoid these hackneyed, "think-time" cliches at all costs.

To collect your thoughts, you can gain two full seconds by just remaining silent. You can pick up another second by using the questioner's name. You can buy up to three more seconds by saying, "Let's see what's at issue here," or by repeating the question, or by asking the individual to repeat it—as long as repeating the question will not reinforce something you don't want reinforced.

In your response, you should avoid using such prefaces as, "Well, as I said before. . . ," or, "I thought I answered that question already, but. . . ." These may give you an extra split second to think, but they come across as rude to all questioners—reporters and audiences alike. Such phrases seem to imply: "Why didn't you listen the first time?"

So, when a questioner asks something that could evoke a negative response from you, how should you react? Give them something they are not prepared for: a calm, courteous, and cooperative attitude—capped off with a positive point about your subject. In anything in life it is important to emphasize the positive. This advice is valid for answering a question from anyone. No matter how unfriendly the question might be, you should respond with a positive attitude and a positive point.

Since the seeds for most follow-up questions are planted within your answers, the more you redirect negatives into positives, the more quickly you will guide the individual away from his or her negative approach toward constructive questions that naturally follow from your positive answers.

When you sense that an individual is trying to set you up for an argument, strike only at the *issue,* never at the person. When you do this, you confound the questioner's expectation of being able to predict the attitude with which you might have responded. This could leave them confused about how to proceed, thus creating an opportunity for you to lead the discussion toward a more constructive direction. Give such questioners something positive, and follow your statement up with examples, illustrations, quotes, dramatic statistics, or whatever will make your answer more interesting.

Conversational answers keep the situation from becoming confrontational. Soon, "baiting" individuals will have to abandon their negative approach, or risk losing their own credibility. For them to continue would be like trying to shadow box in the main ring when they had promised the audience a championship event.

To keep your own feelings under control, always try to address the question, not the questioner. Ignore the techniques being employed, and go directly to the issue. Remember, there are no bad questions—only the potential for bad answers, until you learn how to score positive points.

Through rehearsal and training, you can learn how to take complete charge of yourself and of your answers. No one can make you angry. No one can make you defensive. No one can put words in your mouth. People can only do to you what you are willing to allow them to do.

Questioners and What They Ask

For more than a quarter-century, I have monitored questioners and the roles they play when they ask questions. While you may want to add to this list, the following five roles are the ones that I have encountered most frequently during Q&A sessions and in conference workshops. By recognizing the roles questioners play when they ask questions, we have another tool with which to hone our skills in handling questions successfully.

Here are the five:

SUPPORTERS

These individuals agree with your position. Often, when you call on them, they respond with a supportive comment rather than a question. If they do ask a question, it often leads into a positive point you would like to make. Frequently, supporters give you a direct opportunity to elaborate on points that you have already conveyed. Accept their support graciously, and build on it.

NEGATORS

Although some will feel they have a valid reason for disagreeing with you, negators also include many people who are your basic fault-finders and nay-sayers. When they criticize, acknowledge them with a nondefensive, "understanding" statement, such as: "I understand your feelings on this, and [never use "but," even if it sounds more logical]. . . ." Then say what you prefer to have the audience hear.

DETAILERS

Detailers, like Sergeant Joe Friday, just wants the facts—and as many facts as possible. Indeed, they want all the facts you are willing and able to provide. If you let them, detailers can detail you to distraction. Respond to the question, but make sure that your answer stays at a level that ensures that other members of the audience remain tuned in.

FILIBUSTERERS

When you encounter filibusterers, you know it, often before they ever raise their hand to be recognized—if they even bother to raise their hand. They don't even know the meaning of a question mark. A few may mean well, but under either the stress of asking their "question" or because they suddenly find themselves the focus of the audience's attention, they somehow end up making speeches instead.

About 30 seconds into their monologue, you will sense that you have a filibusterer before you. At that point, listen carefully to their train of thought, note their specific words, and prepare to intervene quickly. The way to handle this is to snag one or two of their key words even as they speak them. Then start talking with the word "and," as though you had been talking all along, and drop in their name right behind the key words.

For example, if your topic happened to be synthetic soles for shoes, and they were droning on about bonding methods as alternatives to stitching, you might catch them in midsentence with ". . . adhesive bonding. . . ." As you do, say, ". . . and *adhesive bonding,* Fred, is something we are all concerned about." Keep on talking until Fred gets the point and trails off. Never look at him again. The audience will thank you for your courage.

WANDERERS/DRIFTERS

Perhaps they drift off the subject, or perhaps they don't even know what the subject is. Wanderers are often in their own worlds. Bring them back on track gently. Your technique for responding to them should be a milder, kinder version of what you would use on a filibusterer.

How to Make Positive Points

There are several ways to assert yourself and make positive points for your organization and its position when you are being questioned. Here are the ones that provide ready opportunities to succeed. When the questioner:

- Asks an easy question.
- Pauses more than five seconds.
- Compliments you or your organization.
- Asks any question that allows you to bridge to your point.

PREPARING YOUR POSITIVE POINTS

Knowing where the opportunities exist for making positive points is one thing, being armed with them ahead of time is another. For example, when a manager prepared to face his company's management committee with a proposal to replace a fleet of trucks that was rapidly becoming obsolete, he jotted down several positive points that included an improved ability to keep trucks on the road, reduced costs of maintenance, lower insurance costs, an attractive image for the company on the road, and driver safety. The committee accepted his proposal, and he told me afterward that he felt that drawing from his storehouse of positive points was a major factor in his success. "In fact," he said, "after I answered one particularly tough question, there was absolute silence. For an instant, I started to feel the old negative emotions surfacing, but I remembered what you had told me. I switched my way of thinking about that silence and looked at it as an opportunity to stick in another positive point. I did, and the follow-up question was supportive—just as you had predicted."

If you want to seize every possible opportunity to make positive points during your Q&A sessions, you will need to be equally well-prepared. Each time you prepare to respond to questions, consider these subject areas and how they might relate to your topic and to the questions you might receive. Then write in your own statements under each heading.

How your plan, project, program, proposal, or whatever, will affect the following in a positive way:

- Your organization
- Its employees
- Its suppliers
- Its method of doing business
- Its customers
- Its profits (or income)
- Its contributions to society: financial, people skills, innovations.

Here are some hints that might help you develop specific content rather than generalities. Consider competitive wages, good benefits, longevity, continuity of employment, job security, promotion from within, equal opportunity, maintenance programs, safety record, environmental safeguards, ethics, security, testing, monitoring, contributions, scholarships, donated facilities, loaned executives, etc. Keep your point brief and specific. Relate each one to the particular interests of your audience. Give examples. Show the value to your own organization or department, as well as to others. (By addressing your self-interest, you heighten your credibility.)

Your "Worst Fears" Questions

Just as it pays to arm yourself with positive points, you can also profit by developing a list of the most difficult questions you can possibly think of.

Consider questions on your topic that might be most critical of the points you plan to make, or the conclusions you plan to draw. Next, write down the relevant tough questions that have troubled you in the past. Finally, dig into your bag of horrors, and write out those questions that you hope and pray no one will ever ask you—about anything that is even remotely likely to be asked.

Don't spare yourself. Go back to the examples of questioners' techniques, and phrase your own tough questions in the worst possible way. Just doing this will help you to stay calmer if any of these kinds of questions are asked.

Now, ask yourself the questions one at a time. Do so in the meanest, toughest way possible. Be ruthless. You may even smile to yourself as you go through the exercise because you will come to realize that none of those ploys can affect you unless you let them. No matter what words questioners use, and no matter how they use their voices, you are in charge—of both your own attitude and answers.

Finding Out What You Need to Know

Many exchanges between presenters and questioners go awry because the participants assume that the other person will know what they meant or that *they* know what the other person was trying to say. Most of the problems occur when the words used can have more than one meaning, no meaning, or any meaning the speaker or listener chooses to assign to them. This is especially true during Q&A periods in which the situations that follow frequently arise. These examples and suggestions should help you respond in a way that produces better communication for everyone:

WHEN INFORMATION IS MISSING
Statement: "Your organization is not very service oriented."
Probe concept: What, specifically makes you feel that way?

WHEN YOU DON'T KNOW TO WHOM OR TO WHAT THE SPEAKER IS REFERRING
Statement: "I find this hard to believe."
Probe concept: What are you having difficulty with?

WHEN YOU DON'T KNOW WHAT IS BEING COMPARED
Statement: "I liked the other way better."
Probe concept: Better than what? In what way?

WHEN THE ACTION IS NOT CLEAR
Statement: "You discourage a lot of initiative."
Probe concept: How do you mean that? In what way?

WHEN THE QUESTIONER TURNS A PROCESS INTO AN EVENT
Statement: "The committee has made its decision."
Probe concept: In your view, what criteria got them there?

WHEN THE QUESTIONER "READS MINDS"
Statement: "Everyone believes this."
Probe concept: How can we tell what *everyone* thinks?

WHEN THE SOURCE OF THE BELIEF OR OPINION IS UNCLEAR
Statement: "They say this is the right way."
Probe concept: Who says this? According to whom?

WHEN THE CAUSE AND EFFECT ARE UNCLEAR
Statement: "Public opinion is going to create problems."
Probe concept: How is that likely to happen?

WHEN IMPERATIVE STATEMENTS ARE MADE

Statement: "We need to [must, have to, cannot, are unable to, etc.] put an end to. . . ."
Probe concept: What would happen if we didn't?

WHEN THE STATEMENT IS OVERBLOWN

Statement: "You people are always saying things like that."
Probe concept: Always? Who else said it? Under what circumstances?

To prepare yourself for specific situations, review each of these examples, and then replace the general statement with one you are likely to encounter. Then, examine the probe concept for each one, and write out your response. Phrase each statement, so that it will be most acceptable to you and to the listener.

If you have experienced other communications obstacles that are not included here, write them down, and go through the same process. This will help you prepare to deal with future situations that may have frustrated you in the past.

Capitalizing on Questioners' Verbal and Non-verbal Cues

When people want to interrupt a presenter, they will frequently start to raise their hands, but many will not carry the gesture through. Instead, they may move their hand into contact with an eye, an ear, their mouth, their other hand, either arm (or even the speaker's arm)—without being conscious of having done so.

When I first noticed this phenomenon, I decided to test it in my seminars. After doing so in over 100 programs on public speaking, involving more than 500 participants over two years, I have come to believe that this phenomenon is connected to the well-researched observations that when people think, sort ideas, or process information—or when they speak with others—they primarily use one of three senses (visual, auditory, or kinesthetic [V–A–K]). This extensive observation led me to conclude that audience members' non-verbals could be used to make reasonably accurate predictions about questioners' representational modes just by noting their hand signals.

WHERE THE HAND LANDS

I found that when listeners start to raise their hands, and then inhibit this "interruption gesture," the place where their partially raised hands either point to or make contact with indicates the representational sys-tem (V–A–K) they are using at that time. For example, if the hand approaches or touches the eye, the person is most likely thinking, sorting, or processing information in a visual mode. If the hand approaches or touches the ear or mouth, the person is most likely thinking in an auditory mode. If it approaches or touches the other hand or either arm, the person is likely to be in a kinesthetic mode.

When listeners inhibit their "interrupt" gesture, and you wish to invite them to make a point or ask a question, start your response with parts of speech that correspond with the mode they have displayed. If Mary's hand went to her eye, for example, you might ask, "How does that *look* to you, Mary?"

We found that when we mismatched a questioner's mode by asking, for instance, "How does that *sound* to you?" or, "Do you *feel comfortable* with that?" the hesitant questioner might be reluctant to respond, or even have difficulty replying. They often even displayed mild frustration with the verbal exchange (not necessarily with the content of what we had said).

Many listeners, when addressed in a mode other than the one they had displayed through their non-verbals, appeared not even to realize that they had signaled an intention to speak. Yet, when we rephrased our question, using the mode they had indicated with their gesture, they often responded.

Take this example: George inhibited a hand-raising gesture, and then tugged his ear. Our initial response: "Doesn't that *appear* accurate to you, George?" George's response: "Oh, I didn't have anything to say about it one way or the other." Our in-mode response: "Oh, I just wanted to be sure that *sounded* okay to you." (Pause.) George then replied almost at once: "Well, actually, now that you *say* that. . . ."

As this example shows, what listeners do with their hands when they approach or contact one of the sense-related body parts can reveal even more. The nature of the contact may even signal that listeners disagree with, or are having difficulty with, your comments.

We found, for example, that people who don't actually make contact, but only "point" toward their eyes, ears, mouth, or other hand or arm—or those who use light, or brushing, hand contact—are generally "friendly" or "supportive" in their comments or questions. Thus, when you see this kind of contact, you can assume (initially, at least) that the listener only wants you to clarify a point, or wishes to support—or add to—a point you just made.

Verbal Approaches That Work

If you wish to engage such questioners, these responses will have the best chance of eliciting a positive, initial rapport:

Hand to eye—"How does that *look* to you, John?"

Hand to ear or mouth—"Does that *sound* okay to you, Jane?"

Hand to hand or arm—"Are you *comfortable* with that, Bob?"

If contact is made, and with intensity—say with rubbing, digging, tugging, grasping, or twisting—you can initially assume that the questioner may disagree with you, or may wish to challenge your point. You could bypass such individuals, but, in doing so, you will lose the opportunity to deal with the matter directly.

A better alternative would be to use one of these responses:

Hand to eye—"Apparently you don't see it that way, John?"

Hand to ear or mouth—"Doesn't sound right to you, Jane?"

Hand to hand or arm—"Are you wrestling with that one, Bob?"

Observing audience members' inhibited hand gestures can help you establish rapport with your listeners when other input is not available. However, the technique provides indicators, not absolutes, so use it only as a guide.

How to Enhance Rapport

You can use a questioner's non-verbals in yet another way to help you achieve better harmony with them. Called "bridging," the technique enables you to observe and reflect a person's own words, voice tones, body language, and other patterns, and then have them flow smoothly with you from one communications mode or channel (V–A–K) to others.

Start by adjusting your own behavior to reflect the questioner's present mode—whether indicated through verb choices, speech rate, breathing, or in any other manner. Then, begin with readily agreeable, general observations, and observe the person's responses. Again pace their verb choices, speech rate, breathing, and other responses. Then switch to another sensory mode.

Once more, observe the questioner's response. Match that again, and then switch to another mode. You should be able to achieve more understanding and acceptance of your point once you have successfully engaged all three modes.

Here are some additional hints that may help you with special situations: If the questioner fails to make the switch with you, or if you observe resistance or lack of interest at any point, immediately shift back to the original mode where interest was high. If you encounter objections, acknowledge the concern directly, then shift back. If the person is indecisive, return to where receptivity was highest and elicit agreement. Then try switching again.

The technique may take more effort than you care to expend, but if you feel that, in the past, you have not received the kind of acceptance you felt was essential for your position or career, you may want to consider the process further. Anthony Robbins' book, *Unlimited Power,* may be helpful to you.

Part Three
Taking Charge of Your *Situation*

I mproving your ability to take charge of the situations in which you are a presenter is your final step toward success. Once you are ready to put all the information you have learned in Parts One and Two into practice, you need only learn how to adapt to each physical setup for maximum success.

In this part, we will explore such important considerations as the layout, lighting, and even the temperature of the rooms in which you present information. You will learn how to check each room and make it your own, how seating arrangements can indicate power positions (and what to do with that knowledge), how risers and platforms affect your presentation, how to use lecterns and microphones, and how to make audiovisual equipment work for you.

You will also learn how to handle special situations that can arise during internal meetings, panel discussions, and videoconferences, and how to present information most effectively on audio and videotape.

Although this is the last part of this book, its position merely follows one's logical flow in the process. In terms of importance, we have saved neither the best, nor the least, for last. All three aspects (self, subject, and situation) are equally important. Any lack of proficiency in handling one or more of these three areas will reflect just as heavily on the others.

Think about it: If you have not taken charge of matters having to do with *self,* your performance is bound to suffer, no matter how well you have developed your content, or arranged your meeting room. On the other hand, if you have a weak *text,* or if your *physical arrangements* are not right, either one is bound to affect how you feel about yourself.

So, as you read this section, remember how important it is to hone and balance your skills in all three areas. This alone will help you to achieve the kind of success that may have prompted you to read this book.

As you move into these final chapters, please remember all that we have already covered. If you take a comprehensive approach, you will move closer toward the success you want.

17
Your Presentation Aids

From time to time, you will be working with the "hardware" of the presentations trade. This may include lecterns, microphones, and equipment on which you can write or display information.

Your "aids" should be exactly that—aids. You should use lecterns to hold your text, not to support a leaning body. Use microphones to help your audience hear, not to blast them out. When you need to generate visual material as you talk, consider easels and blackboards. When your talk is more structured, consider projection equipment—recognizing that overhead projectors let you combine the abilities both to write as you speak and to project information on a screen.

How to Choose the Right Equipment

Here are some points to help you select the right aids for your presentation:

LECTERN
Whether you use a floor model or a table-top lectern, the top ledge closest to you should come just about to the level of your breastbone. If the surface on which you rest your notes were any lower, you would have to look down too deeply into your notes. A higher surface might hide you from your audience. Either raise or lower the lectern, or put a platform behind it.

MICROPHONE

How you use a microphone can make the difference between a polished and an amateurish presentation. There are several types of microphones, all of which can be wired or wireless.

All microphones should be positioned about an inch above a shirt pocket or the handkerchief pocket of your jacket. On men's and women's shirts, the mike will align with the space between the second and third button below the neck. This positioning should give you a good voice level when you speak. Other types of shirts and blouses may have different button arrangements, and you will have to use the hand-span technique that follows to ensure proper placement: Spread your fingers wide apart, look straight ahead, and touch your thumb to your chin. The microphone belongs at the bottom of your little finger. That will put it close enough to pick up your voice properly, while screening out other sounds. When you use any microphone, never walk in front of the loudspeakers, or you will get feedback in the form of whistles or screeches.

Affixed to the Lectern   If you are speaking at a lectern, the microphone may be mounted on a "gooseneck" affixed for this purpose. It may be adjustable, but they are often defective. So do your best to make needed adjustments beforehand, or know how much latitude you will have to adjust it once you are before the audience. Also, do not tap or bump the lectern: The mike may amplify the sound.

Portable   Mikes that are "portable" allow you to walk from place to place, whether they are hard-wired or cordless. Prefer cordless if you have a choice because then you won't have to worry about tripping over cords or getting entangled with your other equipment.

However, if the mike you use is hard-wired, and you plan to walk around while you use it, here are two important tips to remember: Pace off the areas to which you need to go during your presentation to ensure that you have enough cord. Also, tie the wire into a loose, overhand knot around your belt or belt-loop. Then, if you happen to walk too far, you will feel a tug at your waist before you have a hand-held mike yanked away from you, garrote yourself with a lavalier mike, or pull a clip microphone off.

If you do walk around, always keep the excess cord behind you. With a little practice before you face an audience, you can learn to "sweep" the loose cord to your "upstage" side (behind you and the audience) before you walk.

Hand-held Mikes   If you use a hand-held mike, request a portable stand on which to rest it when you need both hands free. Some lectern mikes can be hand-held by removing them from their clip at the lectern.

Hand-held mikes are best used by presenters who have considerable experience because—along with everything else—you have to remember to hold them close to your mouth as you speak and to shift them from one hand to another as you gesture or use props, visual aids, pointers, or other equipment.

Other Types   The two other types of microphones you may encounter are the lavalier, which is positioned directly on you by a cord around your neck, and the clip-on, which is attached to your clothing.

Lavalier Mikes   Some people, including some technicians, refer to clip-on microphones as "lavalier" mikes, or "lavs," so be sure to specify which kind you actually want to use. A lavalier mike will have a string or cord (nonelectric) that loops around your neck. Lavalier mikes often put up a fight when you try to put them on or take them off, so avoid using them if possible. If you have no choice, here is how to deal with a piece of equipment that has more problems, in my opinion, than the benefits it affords in return. To put one on, detach the cord from the clip, if possible. If you can't, form it into a loop with no tangles, slide one end of the cord down, much as you would loosen a neckerchief slide, and slip the open loop over your head, being careful not to mess your hair. Now slide the cord back up to tighten it, until you have the microphone about a hand-span beneath your chin. Often the slides on lavalier mikes are jammed and knotted, forcing you to find a way to separate the cord from the clip, put the mike on, and then reattach the cord where you want it.

When you have a cord that refuses to budge, and you have to use that mike, do what you must. As a presenter, politely forego any discussion of the quality of the equipment or the people who expected you to use it. Instead, take action. If necessary, cut the knotted or stuck cord off with a scissors, tie a piece of sturdy string to the mike cord at the base of the microphone, and tape it to the mike itself with electrician's tape to keep the head of the mike facing your mouth.

Clip-on Mikes These are better. Regard them as tie clasps that have a small ornament mounted on their front. Open the clip, and fasten it to the most practical place possible. Here are the preferred positions, in order: your necktie or scarf, the lapel of your jacket, or at the most logical place on your blouse or shirt.

Always conceal the excess wire from a lavalier or clip-on microphone. Bring it in a straight line down to your waist, tuck it into your waistband, and run the excess behind you, under your jacket if you are wearing one.

Cordless Mikes If you use a lavalier or clip-on mike that is cordless or wireless, you will have to clip a small transmitter/battery pack to your waistband. If you use a hand-held cordless mike, its power supply will be located in the part that you hold.

Most cordless mikes have a switch that enables you to turn the mike on and off or to put it on stand-by. Be sure the mike is turned on before you address your audience, and is in the stand-by or off position when you want to speak privately.

Checking Your Audio Level

When you are ready to do a "mike check" to ensure that your voice is properly amplified, avoid the old, "Testing, one-two-three"—especially if some of the audience have arrived early. Instead, say something that will help you to start thinking constructively. The following procedure is effective and easy to follow:

- Say your name.
- Then give your position or title and your organization's name.
- Next, cap that off with a brief, positive point about the topic you are there to discuss.

Here's how it might go:

"Good morning [or whatever is appropriate to the time of day], Fred [or whatever the interviewer's name is]." Then continue with: "I'm John Jones [your name], CEO [your title] of the XYZ Corporation [your company], and I'm here today to talk about [the topic you will present]."

If someone is helping you with the sound system (and you should have help whenever possible), this mike check should be sufficient for him or her to adjust the system accordingly. If your assistant needs more time, continue speaking about your topic, but don't practice your opening lines. Remember, audience members may already be present.

When Mikes Act Up

More than we care to admit, amplification systems go dead or emit peculiar sounds. When either happens, it needs your immediate attention. If you are comfortable doing so, you might break the audience's tension with a quick quip. Here are a few I vaguely remember tossing out under pressure, even as I tried to rectify the problem:

SCREECHING MIKE

"Attention, K-Mart Shoppers. . . ."

Staring at the mike, "Now, if it only knew the words, we could all get rich."

Staring at the mike, "I wonder if it does harmony."

Holding the mike up high as it warbles while screeching, "This is a drill. Will everyone please throw yourselves face down on the floor until the all-clear sounds."

Waving the wire around to look like a serpent, "Can anyone tame this wild beast?!?"

If your system begins screeching, check to see whether you are standing in front of one of the speakers in your system, or whether you are in alignment with another microphone and thus causing feedback. If so, move until the audio output returns to normal. If that doesn't work, shut the system off. If raising your voice is not a practical way to continue, ask your audience members to move closer to you—even if that means shifting chairs and tables, or arranging the room in a new configuration.

DEAD MIKE

"Here *I* am up here *dying,* and the *mike* drops dead."

"Well, at least it died before I did."

"I didn't think I was doing *that* badly."

"Do we have competitors in the room?"

"Does anyone know how to fix this thing—or should I take the hint?"

"If silence were truly golden, we could all just sit here and get rich."

"Rats. Just as I was about to reveal the secret of eternal youth."

If your amplification system goes dead, check the following in this order: Make sure you didn't accidentally hit the off switch on the mike. If the controls for the system are near you (mounted in the lectern, for example), check all the knobs and switches there. See whether you may have loosened the mike from its wire. If your amplifier is located elsewhere, check that next. Finally, if you have used extra cords to extend your mike wire, check each connection. If you can't get the system operational, raise your voice if that would solve the problem, or ask participants to move closer to you as suggested above.

18
Presenting Information Visually

You already know that audiences remember more of what they have seen *and* heard than they do of what they have only heard. You also now know that most people generally interpret life primarily through the visual mode, and that audiences, in particular, tend to respond best to information that is presented visually.

Although many of the early studies on the psychological interpretations of color by Faber Birren and others have since been refuted, most of us can agree that—at least in the general sense—colors do have "meanings" in today's society. For example, switches that control things that are hot or dangerous are almost always red. David Gordon points out that red is considered a warm color, "whether it is the red of a flame, an apple skin, or a drapery." People also see black objects as heavier than green ones, and red objects as closer than blue ones.

Color can also influence us in ways that we might not be aware of. Gordon points out that as early as 1938, researchers found that blue rooms are perceived as "cold," even when temperatures are raised, and that breathing rates increase when people are exposed to red light.

If you are an experienced presenter, and you want to add even more sophistication to your presentation, you might try these techniques, which I have adapted from my ongoing study of the behavioral sciences.

Advanced Techniques

- To diminish a message or negative news even further (say, in a program that contrasts your services with a competitor's), display information about the competitor without color, letting the light "read" through. The absence of color yields a black-and-white effect that tends to downplay that portion of the message.

• As you do this, you can also position "good-news" copy high on the screen, "bad-news" copy low on the screen. Reverse this arrangement when you want to diminish the impact of either the good or bad news.

Using Color Effectively

Did you notice the wave of television commercials in 1988 and 1989 that switched from color to black and white, then back to color. Or did you see those that used color selectively in black-and-white scenes during the same period? Perhaps the first time your television picture turned to black and white, you thought something had gone wrong with your set. Yet, it was a sophisticated "Madison Avenue" technique at work. Since color has a profound impact on our senses, it makes an even stronger impression when it is contrasted with black and white. It is more than a new way to attract attention.

With some exceptions, a black and white image has less ability to stimulate the viewer. Thus, anything that follows it in color will make a stronger impression. A Nuprin © commercial used the concept effectively. The entire commercial was presented in black and white except the two tablets in the actor's hand and the product name at the end. The advertiser, Bristol-Myers, even matched the color of the product with the color used to display the product's name. Audiences remembered the commercial.

The technique need not be limited to television commercials: It can increase the effectiveness of any visual presentation—whether for sales or management meetings, new business presentations, or speaking engagements.

If you would like to adapt this technique to your visual presentations, here are some tips: For overhead presentations, convert the transparent sheets to film negatives. The backgrounds will be black instead of clear, and the words, charts, or illustrations will be clear instead of black. When you want to present negative or neutral information, show the transparencies as they are. Let white light show through onto the black screen. When you want your audience to remember specific content, color the words with marking pens that are made just for transparencies. For maximum impact, use color sparingly because each color you use dilutes the effect. If you plan to use slides instead of overheads in your presentation, you can use the same, basic technique to prepare them.

When your presentation involves flip charts, you can still use the technique, but in a limited way. Put the neutral or bad news in black ink and write with color, sparingly, only for the information you want your audience to remember.

Other Shifts

Besides shifting between color and black and white, presenters can also shift other aspects of visuals— and even auditory components of a message. The objective would be to influence audience acceptance and recall.

Here are several possibilities, whose outcomes have not yet been researched to my knowledge. Nonetheless, each one would clearly affect audience response. Perhaps, in time, those responses will be studied in depth.

Visual Shift From	To
Still	Motion
Distant view	Extreme close-up
Viewer "outside" the picture (such as when watching an image on a screen)	Viewer "inside" the picture or involved
Unpleasant scene	Pleasant scene

Auditory Shift From	To
Silent	Sound
Soft	Loud
Distant	Close
Slow	Fast
Unpleasant sounds	Pleasant sounds

These contrasts help viewers and listeners retain and recall information beyond that of more routine visuals and sounds. The effectiveness of these techniques is based on well-founded theory that involves the neurosciences and how the mind receives and perceives information.

When your message must stand out against an overwhelming number of messages competing for your audience's attention (say, in a videotape or film on safety), these techniques will make your presentation more successful.

Other factors, of course, can also influence what audiences recall. The content of the black-and-white images—and even where and how the images are introduced onto (or removed from) the screen—is also important. In addition, audiences can be influenced by whether the color shift was also accompanied by a shift from motion to still, or from still to motion. The audio content of the message at the time of the shift will also influence audience impact.

This only begins to explore the many possibilities that are available to presenters. Some people are already using them intuitively, but they point to the day when research in the behavioral sciences will show us new ways to use techniques in a more predictable manner.

Let's now consider the tools with which you might plan to apply some of these techniques.

Writing Tools

If you would like to display key words where audience members can see them as you speak, and you don't want to use projectors, you can use flip charts, blackboards, or flannel boards. Since flip charts (easels and pads) are the most widely used audiovisual tool among presenters, we will discuss them in more detail than we will the other kinds of audio-visual aids, including projectors.

FLIP CHARTS

Technically, "flip charts" are prewritten cards (often professionally), prepared on either sturdy cardboard or foam-core board. Presenters do not use them as frequently as they use easels and pads today. Consequently, most people use the term "flip charts" to apply to the latter, and we'll do the same.

Flip charts can be a valuable tool in presenting information to a small audience, say ten or fewer participants. They are flexible and allow you a wide range of versatility and spontaneity. Because they are associated with authoritative messages, they also add prestige or status—and some say, credibility—to your remarks. They help participants remember your points because people retain more of what they *see* and hear than they do of what they only hear. Flip charts can also serve as a prompt for you, as long as you don't read them instead of speaking to your audience.

Flip charts afford considerable flexibility. You can prepare the sheets easily, and you can readily advance from one to the next. The pads and easels can be carried from place to place, and they let you change your presentation readily.

Yet, despite all this good news, most people dislike using them— even though their jobs may require it. How can you ease the pain and become more effective?

For some people, the anxiety begins the moment they even think about having to tear off used sheets or flip them over the top of the easel. A client expressed it this way: "The first sheet goes fine," she said. "Then a corner catches, and the corner rips off the next one. The third sheet looks even worse, and by the time I get to the fourth, it is likely to rip right down the middle. It's embarrassing! Flipping the used sheets over the top is no solution. Half the time, the easel is taller than I am, and I have to practically leap into the air to toss the sheets over the top. Half the time they land right. Half the time *I* land right. There must be a better way."

Indeed, there is. Here are some tips that will help:

PADS
Start with a new pad, or at least a clean, unwrinkled one. This has almost the same impact as a clean, well-pressed shirt or blouse. Be sure there is enough paper on the pad for your presentation.

If you must use an old pad, take a single-edge blade or a cutting tool with a comparable edge, and trim away all residue left by previous speakers. While you have the blade handy, consider this: On the side of the pad farthest from you, put a slit, two-inches long, right through the perforations found at the top of the sheets.

If your pad has been used before, check every sheet that you must use. More than one speaker has been shocked at what appeared on a presumably blank sheet midway through a presentation. One corporate executive didn't check: Four blank pages later, he unveiled a four-letter obscenity.

PAPER QUALITY
The paper should not be porous. Paper with a smooth finish is less likely to soak up ink and "bleed," spreading beyond the letters, and soaking into the pages below. For comparison, newsprint is porous and tends to look off-white. Magazine print is generally less absorbent and is whiter. Try to obtain the better quality.

If you can't change pads and are stuck with the pens you have, try this: Write quickly, lightly, and only on every other sheet. This will increase the chances that your next writing surface will be free of bleed-through.

TEARING OFF THE SHEETS

Remove each sheet or flip it over as soon as it is no longer relevant to what you are saying. If you're a "ripper" not a "flipper," as you finish with each sheet, consider this advice—a direct steal from Superman's © most famous line: "Up, up, and away!" Reach across to the far top corner of the sheet with both hands, and start the tear if you have not already scored these corners with a sharp blade. Then, with the hand closest to the lectern, pull the sheet along the perforation slowly and carefully toward you with three smooth tugs, lifting up slightly as you pull. The pages should rip off neatly. "Up, up, and away."

DISPOSING OF THE SHEETS

How should you dispose of the used sheets? Crumpling distracts audiences. Instead, fold each sheet in half twice with a light crease. Then place it on the floor behind you, away from where you will be walking.

FLIPPING PAGES

If you plan to flip the pages rather than tear them, be sure you can reach higher than the top of the pad, comfortably. If not, it will help to have an adjustable easel that lets you lower the pad beforehand. Otherwise, your paper may fold and bunch up as you try to "toss" each sheet over the top.

If the easel can only be set at one height, request a small riser that you can step on when you turn a page. Even a sturdy crate, covered with a sheet or tablecloth, will do. If you use one, you'll have plenty of company.

When the Republican National Convention was held in Detroit in 1980, I'm told that workers behind the dais slipped a carpeted cola crate up to the lectern for Senator Tower—then the shortest man in the Senate—just as he took his final step. From backstage, it may have been a primitive way of dealing with the problem, but evidently it worked, and the audience never knew.

Finally, whether you turn or tear each page as you speak, avoid turning your back to the audience. They deserve as much eye contact as you can give them.

THE EASEL

Easels are often flimsy and are notorious for skidding, collapsing, and toppling over. Secure the legs to the floor with duct tape. Don't wait for an embarrassing experience before taking this precaution. In fact, if your pad is loose in its mounting, tape that down too.

Where should you set your easel? Align it, so that both you and the audience can see the pad from your respective positions with a minimal loss of eye contact between you. As a courtesy to your audience, position the easel on the side opposite your writing hand, so that you won't have to cross in front of it or block what you are writing. If you are right-handed, place the easel to your left; if you are left-handed, place it to your right. This will also save you a few steps when you need to walk to it.

MARKING PENS

Use only brand-new, wide marking pens that have felt or porous-plastic tips. Select only the best available. Better yet, bring your own. Use no more than three colors: Black, red, and blue are good selections. New or not, test each beforehand.

Have at least four pens in each color you plan to use. Put two of each color at your easel, and the remainder on the table or lectern from which you will be working. Many presenters tend to walk away from the easel, pen in hand, and leave it elsewhere.

Cap each pen each time you finish writing with it. They dry out quickly. Put the markers down when you are not using them. They make tempting—and distracting—toys. I once watched a presenter hold the cap in his mouth like a pipe or a cigar as he wrote. Thoroughly involved in what he was saying, he absent-mindedly attempted to push the felt tip back into the cap that was still between his lips. He missed, and stuffed the pen up his nose. This may not happen to you, but more than one person has admitted to having put an uncapped pen in their pocket or scratching their neck or cheek with it under the stress of presenting.

Prewritten Talks

If you plan to write your talk on flip-chart pages beforehand, start with a blank cover sheet. This will keep the audience's attention on you during your opening remarks. Put only the title of your talk on your next sheet, and display that sheet as you announce your topic.

The next sheet should be blank, so that the audience will focus back on you until you are ready to direct their attention to the flip chart again. In fact, put a blank sheet between each section of your talk and at any point at which you want the audience to look at you. Remove messages once they are no longer relevant.

Replace prewritten flip charts once they begin to show the first signs of wear. To do otherwise compares with showing up in a shirt or blouse you dug out of your dirty laundry.

Writing Tips

• Keep your message concise: Limit each sheet to one thought and to about four to seven words per line. Write no more than nine lines on a page, but six or seven would be better, since research has shown that people can only absorb seven bits of information at a time, plus or minus two. Put only one idea or concept on each sheet.

• Write as high as practical on the sheets, and leave lots of room at the bottom, so that participants can see the information better.

• Use block letters, not script. Write on an even plane—even if you have to draw rules in light pencil beforehand.

• Make your letters at *least* an inch-and-a-half high—especially if more than ten people need to see your information.

• Spell all words correctly. Errors in spelling imply other errors in your talk.

• Never apologize for your handwriting or your "artistry." People want information, not excuses. Focus on content, not on your method of conveying it.

Using Color

Use color judiciously to help your audience distinguish among the major points and to help them see how your subordinate points support each main idea. One approach would be to list all your major points in blue and your supporting ideas in black—reserving red for the "hot" points that you want to emphasize. Keep each page in a single color, unless you need a second color for contrast or dramatic impact.

Two Easels?

If you have a lot to write, and you want to leave the information where the audience can see it for cross-reference, consider using two easels. Otherwise, carry masking tape with you, so that you can tack the sheets up, and make certain you have an appropriate place in which to hang them. (Plastic tape may not hold.)

Delivery Style

Let each graphic *support* your point, not *duplicate* it. Thus, if you wrote "Budgetary Analysis" on your pad, the words you speak should be different. For example, you might say, "I would like to show you how we arrived at these figures." This is far better than saying, "And now for the Budgetary Analysis." Or, worse yet, "As the next sheet shows, we are going to talk about the Budgetary Analysis next."

Varying the words you speak from the words in your visual aids helps keep the audience's attention. Avoid referring to the visual aids themselves: "As the next sheet shows" distracts from your message. Such phrases bore audiences.

When you present flip-chart information, be sure to look at your audience. If you face the pad when you talk, the audience may not hear you, and it will be more difficult for you to maintain your enthusiasm and sincerity.

Here's a step-by-step process that works: Say whatever the audience will need to hear as you turn to the next sheet; glance at it to cause audience members to do the same; then look back at the audience as you continue to speak. Repeat this for every sheet.

BLACKBOARDS
Have two, if possible. Erase one with a damp sponge, and, as it dries, write on the other. Have plenty of extra, *new* chalk, and break about one-third off each piece *before* you use it. Then it will be less likely to snap in your hand while you are writing.

FLANNEL BOARDS
Seasoned speakers don't use them, although the products still appear in the catalogs. Consider the alternatives, instead.

Projection Tools

OVERHEAD PROJECTOR

The equipment can be advantageous for many presentations. However, first the drawbacks: It requires a screen; it projects glaring light; and it generally has a noisy, high-powered cooling fan that blows away anything in its range.

Overhead presentations offer a great deal of flexibility: They enable you to overlay successive transparencies and to write directly on the transparency material. The transparencies are also relatively inexpensive to make. In fact, many copy machines can produce them.

If you plan to use an overhead projector often, and for the same talk, the tips that follow will help to improve the impact of your visuals and help you become a more effective speaker.

• Convert the transparencies into film negatives, and color in the words and illustrations. A photographer can make the negatives, and a stationery store can provide the color markers. The negatives eliminate the distracting glare and help your audience focus on your message.

• When you change transparencies, lay a solid negative, or even a piece of thin cardboard, over the one you want to remove. Position your next transparency over that. Then slide the "blackout" sheet away. You may need to modify the blackout sheet for some equipment.

• Key your colors according to the major headings and subheadings of your presentation. Use colors that are consistent with your message. For example, you might want to display good news in green, neutral news in blue, and negative news in red—though not if you want to diminish the impact of the bad news.

• If your presentation builds audience acceptance with each subsequent point, advance colors according to their "temperature," beginning with the cool colors and leading up to the warmer ones (e.g., blue-green-yellow-orange-red).

• When you build up several points into a group over a series of transparencies, display each new point in a fresh, vivid color, and put all previous points in whatever "standard" color you have chosen for that part of your presentation.

SLIDE PROJECTORS

Slide presentations can be effective, especially when the audience is too large to see a flip chart or blackboard comfortably. However, slide presentations are difficult to change on short notice and are still somewhat costly and time-consuming to make, although new computer techniques have reduced the costs and simplified the job. Many of the same suggestions made for overhead projection apply here.

FILMSTRIP PROJECTORS
I don't recommend these because they are difficult to use when you need to key your visuals to your talk. Film strips are best used in educational environments with the audio track keyed to each frame advance.

MOTION-PICTURE PROJECTORS
If you must show a film, remember that the equipment is noisier and even more cumbersome than overhead or slide projectors are—and less flexible than either.

VIDEOTAPE MONITORS
Video technology has advanced rapidly. However, as visual aids, videotapes lack flexibility. You can use prerecorded videotapes in your presentations with some control. For example, you can start, pause, and stop more easily than you could with a film or film strip. The image you display on your screen must be large enough for everyone in the audience to see, or you will need to provide additional monitors.

When you have time to prepare beforehand, you might still use
You can also use video equipment when you plan to rely on flip charts, but find that your audience is too large to see them. Simply point a video camera at the chart, and project the information through television monitors. Since the flip charts' ratio of height to width won't match that of the television screens, whatever is around or behind your easel will take up the rest of the screen, so be sure it does not distract from your message.

When you have time to prepare beforehand, you might still use television to project your visuals, but in this way: Put your information on sturdy card stock (17" × 22" is a good size), and simply have the camera operator project each visual onto the monitor screens whenever you display one.

You can also generate visuals through an interface between computers and video monitors. However, this requires a considerable amount of equipment on location. It is cumbersome for those who have to travel, and requires too much preparation to be useful in creating visuals on the spot. Consider the other ways to use television instead.

Checklist

I developed the following checklist for my own use. Consequently, it lists each item according to my most frequent use of it, or according to its priority in most of my presentations and seminars. Since every presenter should develop his or her own checklist, adapt this one to suit your own specific needs.

EQUIPMENT NEEDS

Video

_____ TV monitor(s)   (minimum size _____)

_____ TV camera(s)   _____ Tripod(s)—(on wheels preferred)

_____ VCRs—½″ VHS format

_____ Teleprompter(s) (descr. _____)

Other Electrical or Electronic Equipment

_____ Overhead projector

_____ Spare blank transparency sheets   _____ Extra frames

_____ Slide projector   _____ Remote control (prefer cordless)

_____ Screen   Size: _____

_____ Extension cord(s)   Length: _____

_____ Microphone(s)   _____ Microphone stand(s)

    Type: Type:

    _____ Hand-held   _____ Table

    _____ Clip-on   _____ Lectern

    _____ Neck-type   _____ Floor

_____ Microphone cord(s)   Length: _____

_____ Lectern—with light, if needed

_____ Other: telephone(s), floodlights, etc. _____

Visual Aids

_____ Easel   _____ Pad—prefer new

_____ Marking pens
        Colors: black/red/third color

_____ Blackboard(s)   _____ Chalk—prefer new

_____ Eraser(s)   _____ Bucket of water and sponge

Other Items Needed

_____ Raised platform
        (Min.—12ft. × 24ft.)

_____ Chairs

        _____ For audience   _____ For "studio" set

_____ Tables

        _____ Rectangular for audience
              Seat 2–4, facing front

        _____ Low table for "studio" set

        _____ Table for coffee service

_____ Props (for "set")

        _____ Plants   _____ Drapes

        _____ Other

_____ Coffee Service

        _____ Coffee   _____ Tea (or hot water
                                       and tea bags)

        _____ Milk and sugar (plus artificial sweetener)

        _____ Cups, saucers, spoons, napkins

        _____ Soft drinks, iced tea, juices

        _____ Glasses for soft drinks

_____ Bite-sized pastries or snacks
(no powdered sugar)

_____ Fresh fruit   _____ Other _____

_____ Signs

_____ No Smoking Please   _____ No Entrance

_____ Quiet Please,   _____ Other _____
Recording in Progress

19
Physical Arrangements

Whether you are presenting information internally or speaking before an outside audience, you will still find that every meeting room has its own dynamics, reflected largely by its layout and physical aspects. This is so true that you can learn a lot about a room—even when it is empty.

Many indicators can reveal a room's "power," and you can learn to read the signs with very little practice. In fact, these tips will enable you to walk into an empty room and determine how much "authority" it has and where the highest-ranking individual will sit. That knowledge can help you to make certain adjustments—physical or attitudinal—that will help improve your presentation even further.

LAYOUT
Where is the table (or tables) in relation to the doors? How many doors are there? Generally, a room with only one door will enable you to locate the room's "power" area more quickly. When there are two doors, where do they lead? Does one go to a hallway? Does the other open into an area leading to executive offices? How much space is there between the table(s) and the walls? Is the spacing uniform? Are the chairs evenly spaced around the table(s), or are they more loosely spaced in one area?

The area where the table is farthest from the wall and where the chairs are the most widely spaced will indicate the power spot. Also, the door will generally face the top official, so that he or she can see who's coming and going.

LIGHTING

Is the room bright or dim? Are the lights exposed or recessed, fluorescent or incandescent? A power room will have recessed lighting from incandescent bulbs—often in the form of floodlights around the edges of the room.

FURNISHINGS

Are the tables hardwood or plastic? Are the plants live or artificial? Is the floor carpeted or tiled? Are the wall decorations originals or prints? Are the chairs on castors with swivels, or upright? Are they covered with fabric or vinyl?

A power office will have hardwood tables, live plants, carpeting, original artwork, and fabric-covered chairs that roll and swivel. You may also find such obvious power symbols as a desk set or a telephone. If the phone is located on the table, near where the top official will sit, most participants will not use it to make calls unless the leading executive tells them to do so. If it is located at a table near the top person, meeting participants will be more likely to use it, but may still ask permission.

If you can alter the power center of any room in some way, it will generally be to your advantage to do it. For example, you might put the table closer to the wall on the power side, or add more chairs to that side of the table. This shifts the balance somewhat in your favor and gives you a little more control as the presenter.

Some time ago, I set up a training session in a board-room-type facility. There were two doors. One led to a hallway, the other to the "executive suite." The room was clearly set up with the power at that end, as indicated by better lighting, more space, better artwork, and so on.

To provide more room for videotaping, I had the table moved to that end of the room and placed crossways. Then we set four chairs (one for each participant) on one side, one chair at one end for the coordinator of the meeting, and one on "my" side of the table for me. At the other end of the table, we placed a lesser chair for the person who was to operate the video camera for me. Then I closed the door behind me and hung a sign on the outside that read: "Seminar in Progress—Use Other Door."

When the executives came through "their" door, they immediately commented on the shift, and *then* settled in for coffee—still commenting on the shift. When the two lower-ranking managers (only two levels down from the others) came in—through the executive door—they actually knocked, even though the door was open. They immediately went to the empty end of the room ("their" end) before returning for coffee—rooms have power, indeed.

Through countless, conscientious efforts at arranging many kinds of rooms to ensure that my seminars are as effective as they can be, I now automatically do certain things. In a restaurant, I never sit with my back toward a door, I won't accept a table near a serving station where water and utensils are stored, and (if I am hosting the meal) I always try to sit where I can catch the server's eye quickly.

When I ride on a train or plane, I sit on the aisle to have more room to stretch out. When three people have to sit in the back seat of a car or taxi, I always hold the door for the first two, ensuring myself an outside seat. In any meeting, I try to arrive at the room ahead of others, so that I will have the seat of my choice. You can do the same—and you should.

Seating Arrangements and Power Positions

Within certain bounds, you can allow your presentation to determine the best way to arrange your room, using the formats in the accompanying diagram. Some "rules" can help you do this.

• If your purpose is to entertain, you can use a theater-style format. Generally participants will not need tables.

• If you are there to inform, you can still set up theater style. However, a classroom arrangement might be better. Provide tables when participants will need to take notes.

• If your objective is to instruct or train, you can use either the classroom arrangement or a herringbone (chevron-style) plan. The chevron setup focuses the audience members more directly on you and on each other. Provide tables for participants.

• Panel discussions require a table for the panel members, perhaps a separate position, such as a lectern, for the moderator, and a theater or classroom seating arrangement for the audience.

• Use several round tables when you require little focus on yourself and need participants to work together in small groups. This would be the case when you want each group to work on the same (or different) specific aspects of a given problem.

• Banquet seating, of course, should be reserved for presentations at which a meal will be served. Try to avoid speaking from where you eat.

If possible, persuade the host to provide a lectern that is separate from your dining table.

In all these cases, you will deliver your presentation in front of the audience. However, in a problem-solving meeting, where you need the most audience participation possible, consider a conference-style seating arrangement. You can use an oval, a circular, or a rectangular table, or you can form several tables into a closed rectangle. Avoid setting up tables, so that they form a square hole in the center. The hole serves no purpose and wastes space.

Meetings for solving problems might also take place around two tables in a "T" arrangement or, if space is limited, in an "L." You could also arrange three tables in a "U" configuration.

All three layouts risk placing people with their backs to you, and the areas where right angles form will be the least comfortable. Discourage anyone from sitting where either problem might occur.

In a "T" layout, speak from the "head-table" part of the setup, or, if that is not possible, operate from the "foot" of the letter. A skilled presenter can actually turn this into a second power position. In an "L," work from either end of the letter, with the most powerful or influential audience members facing you. A "U," again, gives you a "head-table" effect. Work either from that area or from the "tops" (in this case, actually "bottoms") of the letter. Prefer the side that is farthest from the door if the door is at that end—which it is likely to be.

The criteria discussed at the beginning of this chapter, along with such physical constraints as the location of a fixed screen or wall easel, may dictate the most effective spot from which to deliver your presentation. However, you might be able to make further changes by bringing in portable screens and easels, regardless of the permanent fixtures provided.

Risers and Platforms

When you seat more than 40 people at the same level, a riser may help them see when you need to conduct demonstrations, use props, or employ certain visual aids (such as a flip chart that you can use for up to 50 people if you write in large letters and put only a few words on a sheet). Risers put you physically and psychologically "above" the audience and tend also to distance you from participants. So be aware of these implications, and do what is appropriate for your role, your topic, and the occasion.

Make certain that the riser or platform is large enough to accommodate all your needs. Be sure you can fit all your equipment comfortably on it. Allow room for those who will need to walk on and off the "stage."

If others will need to be seated on the platform, know what their roles will be and how much space they will need to do their jobs. Know what they will do once they finish. Try to arrange for them to leave the risers and become part of the audience before you begin. To understand why, imagine what it would be like for entertainers to perform on the "Tonight Show" with Johnny Carson standing right there on camera within ten feet of them throughout their entire performance. Even attentive people who share the limelight tend to distract from your presentation.

Briefing Your Helper

As we saw earlier, it helps to have someone serve as your "gatekeeper." This person may be the same one who introduces you. Ask whether he or she would be willing to help seat people in the front rows first, enforce meeting rules about smoking, eating, and so on, help you with handouts, collect evaluation forms, and deal with disruptive people (who often include hotel staff during outside presentations).

Check Your Room

Arrive at the room where you will speak at least an hour early. Walk around and check out everything. Know where you will stand, how far you can move, and where your equipment should be positioned.

Just giving yourself time to become comfortable in an unfamiliar environment will help you feel calmer and more confident. It's a lesson I learned from an elderly pet-shop owner many years ago. My oldest son and I had just set up a salt-water aquarium and had followed the instructions to the letter. I brought home two expensive tropical fish in a plastic bag, and we poured them into the tank. The next morning, we found them dead, belly-up. I returned them to the shop owner who replaced them and explained how to prevent the problem from recurring. He said to keep the fish in their water in the bag, open the top, and *ease* the bag into the tank. He said the fish could then decide when they were ready to come out. As he put it, "It eliminates the shock. Every living creature needs time to adjust to its environment." The fish lived for years, and

I have been telling presenters for years to avoid *speaker* shock by arriving early and easing into *their* environments.

Once you are in the room, locate the light switches and dimmers. Do the controls enable you to keep light on the audience while you darken the area where you will screen your visuals? Is there enough light for videotaping if that is included in the plans?

Locate the thermostat if the room has its own control. Is the temperature right? Generally, a temperature between 68° and 72° is comfortable for most presentations. Any extremes in temperatures will distract your audience from your message.

Can you control the temperature, or must you ask someone else to adjust it for you? If there are no controls, be prepared to request fans or heaters. It may take time to locate such equipment, which is another reason for checking your meeting room at least an hour before you need to use it. If you can't get what you need, request another room.

Will there be any audible distractions, such as sound coming from an adjacent room? Many years ago, before I learned the wisdom of leaving nothing to chance and having a "gatekeeper" assist me, I had to stop five minutes into a presentation to go to the adjacent room and ask a rock band to postpone their rehearsal until I finished.

Will your audience be free from visual distractions, such as columns and pillars? Again, experience is a great teacher (but experienced teachers can save you headaches). I once walked into my presentation room early to find that several square, mirrored columns were scattered throughout the rather small, corridor-shaped room. People seated near them would be distracted by anything the mirrors reflected—including their own images. Within 15 minutes, we had obtained a roll of butcher's paper and taped over the mirrors from the floor to seven feet up. It wasn't beautiful, but at least the posts were no longer distracting.

To build audience receptivity, Tyler Lorig, a Yale researcher in psychophysiology, has a unique tip (*Prevention,* May 1988): The aroma of certain foods, such as apple pie, can cause brainwave changes associated with the calmness produced by well-known, stress-reduction techniques.

While you might not be able to arrange for pies, you could help your presentation by serving coffee and pastries. The aroma of fresh-perked coffee can relax people even as it "perks" them up. If you do serve coffee, keep it fresh, and offer decaffeinated and tea as alternatives. Make sure the cups, plates, napkins, and utensils reinforce the message you want to convey. Plastic, styrofoam, and paper say something entirely different about your presentation than silver, china, and linen.

When nothing else is possible, consider using one of the spice-scented air fresheners now on the market. Once, I found that the room in which I was to conduct my program was particularly musty and smelled of cigarettes. To get rid of the odor, I had someone locate an air freshener that smelled almost like a pie being baked. I believe it made quite a difference in the receptivity of my audience.

You might consider other ways in which to make your room appear more friendly. Flowers, for example, are always a friendly touch.

Check Your Equipment

Once you are in your room, check every piece of audiovisual equipment you plan to use. Are all the pieces there? Do you have power? Can you put the equipment where you want it, or will you need extension cords?

• Carry a three-pronged adapter and a three-outlet coupler with you. Many meeting rooms lack outlets where you need them. Make sure that all wires on the floor are taped down, so that no one trips and gets hurt, pulls out your power, or knocks over your equipment.

• Set your slide trays, overheads, videotapes, or other visuals where you can reach them.

• Do a test run with each piece of equipment. Make sure you have spare projector bulbs.

• If you plan to use a lectern, check it out. Does the light work? Is it set at the right height? If you are working from a side table (say, for handouts that you give participants as you go along), is everything placed where you can find it quickly?

• Check your microphone. Does it work? If it isn't cordless, can you move where you need to?

• Check the entranceways to your room and the adjacent restrooms that your participants will use. They must be clean because these areas influence people's attitudes and their receptivity to your presentation. If these areas need attention, insist that someone take care of them before your audience arrives.

• Check the chairs and tables. Remove any that are broken or damaged. Make sure the spacing between rows and aisles will provide comfortable passage for handicapped and other participants. Have soiled or torn table covers replaced. A clean, fresh start sets the tone for everything that follows.

Have a Checklist

Before your next presentation, develop your own list of everything you might need before, during, or immediately after your presentation. When you arrive, run through your checklist point by point. Make certain every question or issue you have raised has been dealt with to your satisfaction at least a half-hour before you speak. The more you take charge beforehand, the less that can happen once you begin.

Presenter's Road Kit

Pliers/cutters
Screwdriver (Philips/blade)
White correction fluid
Multipurpose felt marking pens
  (red, black, blue, green)
Nylon tip marking pen
  (black)
Chalk
Grease pencil (for overheads)
Ruler
Transparency film (for
  overheads)
Sewing kit (w/buttons)
Safety pins
Straight pins
Glyoxide(r), Ornex(r)
Lozenges, cough drops

Duct tape
Electrician's tape
Transparent tape
Scissors
Stapler (and staples)
Paper clips (regular and large)
Spring clips
Push pins
Rubber bands (large and
  small)
Glue stick
12 feet of heavy cord
Extension cord (min. 10ft.)
Multioutlet adapter
Three-prong adapter
Spare bulbs (for projectors)
A/V jacks and adapters

20
Special Situations

Most of what you need to be effective and successful in your presentations has already been covered in this book. However, in certain situations—panel discussions, teleconferencing, and delivering your presentation on videotape or audiotape—special "rules" apply. If you follow the advice given for each, you will be far more comfortable, and appear far more polished than most presenters in these same circumstances.

Internal Meetings

First, let's cover a bit more about the psychology of meetings within your own organization, since most of your presentations will probably take place in that environment. We have already talked about the purposes of meetings—to inform, to persuade, to train, and so on. Once you know your purpose, your audience, and the physical environment in which you will speak, you might also want to know more about the dynamics of the group in which you will be presenting information.

The best understanding of how people function within groups—or even as individuals—comes from work done by David McClelland when he was at Harvard. He found that people are motivated to one degree or another by the drives toward power, affiliation, and achievement. McClelland's work has been discussed by Joseph Yeager, head of the Eastern NLP Institute, Newtown, Pennsylvania, in his book, *Thinking about Thinking with NLP.*

POWER (DOMINANCE/COMPETITION/POLITICS)
Some people are motivated within meetings by the opportunity to experience a sense of power or a chance to exercise leadership.

AFFILIATION (RELATIONSHIPS/COURTESY/COOPERATION)
Others may enjoy the opportunities that meetings provide for networking. They welcome the contact with both new and familiar people. Affiliation may mean different things to different executives. Sally may listen. Ted may talk about issues. Fred may promote himself. Tania may try to get on Fred's team.

ACHIEVEMENT (RESULTS/GOALS/OBJECTIVES)
Still others may see meetings as an opportunity to accomplish things, to get something done, or to contribute ideas that will lead to the success of the organization or of themselves.

Clearly, not all meeting climates will be the same, and even knowing whether individual participants are balanced more toward power, affiliation, or achievement may not give you all the information you need. Even a person's "stake" in the outcome of a meeting can influence his or her level of involvement and the intensity with which he or she participates in the discussion.

Trying to come up with a detailed profile for an internal management team and having it apply in all situations would be like trying to profile a professional athletic team and expecting the information to apply in every situation of every game they play. The dynamics change constantly, and the controlling factors would be immeasurable.

Several years ago, Herbert I. Abelson of Opinion Research Corporation described two types of groups you may face: statistical and functional.

STATISTICAL GROUPS
These consist of people classified by age, sex, income, education, occupation, and so on. In general, members of such groups can be expected to respond in much the same way to the same communications—if there is no strong reason to do otherwise. Strictly within the context of groupings, we would have to know more about each individual to determine whether they were more heavily motivated toward power, affiliation, or achievement.

FUNCTIONAL GROUPS

These play more vital roles than statistical groups, however, because they organize in terms of like interests. Typical examples would include construction crews, church congregations, clubs, and volunteer organizations. Members of such groups tend to seek security in their social relationships that may, in turn, lead to collective decision making and action. Without any other input, you can appeal to a functional group in terms of affiliation—and you will recognize how Maslow level three applies here.

Abelson tells us that if you want to change the attitudes of individuals within a functional group, you must first change the group's attitude. The stronger they perceive their affiliation with the group to be, the more difficult it will be to have them act in what they may perceive as conflict with the group's norms.

Of course, within each group, you will have leaders and achievers. By learning who they are and appealing to their specific drives—within the context of what's good for the group—you may increase your chances for swaying group opinion.

In *The Group Workshop,* Douglass discusses the many roles that participants may undertake within a meeting. While I don't agree that people can be labeled so readily, I do agree that all the *functions* described may well take place within any meeting. His labels include: catalyst, clarifier, explorer, formulator, gatekeeper (not as I use the term), mediator, programmer, synthesist, and weigher.

To respond best and use the input from each participant to best advantage, you should know the role that each of your participants is playing at the moment, and add these to the list of "players" we already described in Part Two (supporters, negators, detailers, filibusterers, and wanderers/drifters).

As you can see, especially within internal meetings, the dynamics of groups and of individuals within those groups can be extremely complex. It would be a gross disservice for me to try to persuade you that a few handy "rules" can help you deal with the subject effectively.

Take the time to get to know each person who is likely to participate in meetings in which you are a presenter. Try to learn their styles, their motives. Determine how they filter and process information, and you may be able to predict (with some accuracy) how they might participate in your meetings. Then, try to anticipate their questions, and use the information in Chapter 15 on the Q&A period to prepare yourself to respond to questions they might ask. This additional preparation will make you feel much more comfortable.

Panel Discussions

A panel discussion generally consists of a host and three or four people who have special knowledge about the subject under discussion. Most panels consist of a gathering of colleagues who will share their views before a friendly audience. However, panels often consist of people and audiences who have opposing views.

The host's job is to run the program according to rules that were established and agreed upon beforehand. Generally, the format will consist of an overview by the host, a setting forth of the rules for the audience's benefit, and an opportunity for each presenter to speak for a given period. In some formats, the host will ask the panelists all the questions. However, he or she may also invite questions from the audience and, in some panel discussions, allow panelists to question one another. Generally, the questions will address a specific topic, and departures from the agenda will be discouraged.

A good host does his or her homework well, and generally prepares a list of questions regardless of the format. The panelists will almost always know the topic in advance, and may also be told the subtopics that will be discussed. However, they may not be given the specific questions ahead of time. If you are a panelist, you can rehearse by anticipating the specific questions and practicing the main points you want to make in response. Even during friendly panel discussions, the host may ask a provocative question. This often occurs as part of the natural and logical flow of the exchange and should not be considered a "betrayal."

Because time is generally limited and the agenda fairly structured, your responses to questions will have to be concise, to the point, and clear to everyone. There will be little or no opportunity to amplify or clarify, so it is doubly important to know the positive point or two you plan to make during the limited time you will be invited to speak.

Avoid repeating negative words or concepts or responding defensively. There simply isn't enough time to overcome the impact of this approach. Know the positions and attitudes of your co-panelists. Anticipate their points and, if they conflict with yours, be prepared to express and support your views.

Even when panels are comprised of people who support each other's views, participants or the host may interrupt on occasion—especially if the person speaking is long-winded or "boring." When that happens, the train of thought often shifts to another aspect of the topic at hand or, less frequently, to another topic in a related area. Be prepared for that to happen.

If panelists are given the opportunity to make brief opening statements, be ready with well-organized, concise, positive remarks that support your views. Know how much time you will have, and use it wisely. Because the format may not allow you sufficient time to communicate your point through logical development, you may have to hit only the headlines and hope that you will be able to amplify during the questioning.

When the format allows for dialogue among the panelists, or for them to question one another, stay alert for strategic opportunities to interject a positive point at any time. Consider the techniques I discussed in the material on handling questions in Part Two—especially the technique we talked about for handling filibusterers. You can latch right onto the end of another panelist's response, just as though you were merely finishing his or her sentence.

As you did with the "filibusterer," listen for a key word or phrase in the guest's answer, and then, as soon as he or she pauses, pick up that word or phrase, preceded by ". . . and . . . ," and then continue from there. For instance, if the guest has just said, ". . . in genetic research today," and you want to make a positive point, you can chime in without missing a beat, ". . . and genetic research is something . . . ," and keep right on talking.

As I mentioned earlier, once you start this technique, however, you must push on until you have completed your point. Be brief, so as not to appear rude. However, if the host persists in trying to stop you, then stop immediately.

You can look and feel more relaxed by leaning forward and keeping your hands and arms apart. Keep your body relaxed but attentive. Convey your interest in what is taking place even when you are not speaking.

Look at the person who is speaking or to whom you are speaking—even if that person is not looking at you. This is especially important if the speaker is a colleague or another person who supports your organization's viewpoint. However, it is also a way to keep focused on the dialogue, and it shows the audience that you are courteous.

If the panel consists of antagonists, and a critic is cutting your position to ribbons, you can take action, but you must do it politely. Attract the host's attention by reaching forward with an open hand, or even by gesturing with a pencil or pen, *slightly*. This flags the host, and he or she should get the message—especially if shifting to you will be seen as the right thing to do. The host may not let you interrupt to get your point in, but the gesture has served notice that you have something to say. It almost guarantees that you will be called on for "rebuttal."

If you do get the floor in this manner, be sure not to debate. Instead, crisply score your positive point, and then relinquish the floor to the host or hostess. This technique can be used just once in an interview, so use it judiciously. Pick your best time.

You may have only two or three opportunities to respond to questions in an entire panel interview. Therefore, the words you choose must be right. Be concise. Time is limited. Support your position with facts. Use anecdotes or actual cases to emphasize your points and to help the audience relate to them.

Videoconferencing

Although many organizations have resisted the concept of videoconferencing, it is on the move. Costs have been dropping and more organizations—particularly colleges and universities—have been developing teleconferencing capability. Many schools make their facilities available to outside organizations.

Teleconferencing can be used in many ways, and the equipment needed can range from one-way video and two-way audio to full-video capability at both ends. Some of the applications include news conferences, annual meetings, and seminars.

According to one estimate, more than 15,000 teleconferences were held in 1988 within the United States, and nearly 20,000 sites in this country were capable of receiving videoconferences. By 1988, the costs of renting satellite time were about $300 an hour, down from $2,000 an hour a few years earlier. As more facilities become available for teleconferencing, interest will continue to grow, and more people will use this communications tool to reach remote audiences, perhaps in several locations at one time.

If you plan to participate in a teleconference, there are some special "rules" that go beyond the traditional ones for presenters. To come across as effectively as you would like, the following tips will help:

EYE CONTACT

Maintaining eye contact with the person speaking during a teleconference is one of the easiest ways to help ensure the success of your program. If there is more than one camera at the originating location, the director will most likely have a camera on the questioner, at least one on you, and possibly another to "cover" the broader area. As you are being asked a question from the audience, look directly at the person asking the question until he or she has finished speaking. Continue looking at the questioner when you begin your response. Then, you may "share" your eye contact with the rest of the audience.

Here is the logic: The camera that covers you should show you being attentive at all times, and your eye contact conveys that. Viewers at your other locations will be depending entirely on their video screens to assess your courtesy, sincerity, and other desirable attributes. Your attentiveness is the only measure they have.

Be especially attentive when you are being asked a difficult question. A close shot of you looking up, down, or away would convey a most uncomplimentary image.

If you hired the crew, have the director use medium shots of you while you are listening to the question and when you first begin to respond. Then, should you inadvertantly break eye contact, the situation is not magnified as it would be with an extreme close-up of your face and eyes on the screens.

Once you begin responding to the question, the director can be more flexible in using close-ups of you—perhaps intercut with shots of the questioner or others in the audience. In covering the audience, the director should generally not hold a shot too long on one person because his or her movements could become distracting. The director should also select only those audience members whose eye contact communicates that they are being attentive.

Before the conference, ask the director which camera will be on you when a question comes from one of your "remote" locations. You can usually check this by seeing which camera has a red light on. Once you know the correct camera, look right at it as the questioner is speaking, and continue to look at it as you begin your response.

Here is why: First, the questioner does not have the benefit of seeing you live. You come to him or her only as a two-dimensional image on a television screen. Second, questioners often seek the reassurance, through your non-verbal communication, that you are "listening." This will be especially true when they are trying to ask a question of a person who is not even in the same city.

To illustrate: In a phone conversation, you expect periodic "I see," "Hummm," and "Uh huh" kinds of feedback—otherwise you begin to wonder whether the other person is even listening. This ritualistic behavior is reassuring, and a teleconference caller or questioner needs similar reassurance. If the questioner should happen to see you on screen looking elsewhere, he or she will feel that you are not being properly attentive. By looking directly at the camera, the picture on the screen will show you looking at the questioner. Incidentally, when you do this, *all* viewers will feel that you are looking directly at them.

For the best use of eye contact, look at the person who is speaking, or the person to whom you are speaking. Thus, when the moderator is speaking or inviting questions, you will be seen as giving him or her your undivided attention should the director put a shot of you on screen. Maintain this eye contact, even if you happen to be reaching for a sip of water between responses.

Eye contact is also crucial when one of your colleagues is fielding a question. When you pay attention, the audience is more likely to regard his or her comments as being important.

If you receive a question and want to turn it over to a colleague for a response, announce your intention to do so. Then finish your sentence, and look at the colleague as you finish. This gives your colleague time to collect his or her thoughts. It also gives the director time to widen the shot to encompass both of you, set a camera on the colleague, and make a smooth transition. It also shows you as being courteous to the colleague (as did the early warning that he or she would be asked to answer the question).

Everyone in front of the cameras should look at the person as he or she speaks. You must look interested even if you've heard the answer 100 times before, otherwise the audience will be less likely to give proper value to what is being said.

Caution: Everyone on the dais may have a question turned over to them at any time and should keep their minds tuned in to the person speaking. Nothing is worse than to have your thoughts wander, and then suddenly hear the speaker ask you to respond to a question or thought that you did not even hear. Looking at the speaker helps to block out distractions and keep thoughts focused on the topic being discussed.

Audiotapes and Videotapes

When you deliver your presentation on audiotape or videotape, all of this book's guidance for preparing yourself and your subject will still apply.

However, when you deliver an audiotaped presentation, your gestures and voice dynamics will have to be even more emphatic. Gestures, of course, add more color to your voice, and on audiotape your voice is the only tool you have working for you—other than content. People who listen to speakers on tape are easily distracted by visual stimuli that have nothing to do with your message, and they tend to tune you out more quickly.

TIPS FOR RECORDING AN AUDIOTAPE
These tips will help make your audiotape more memorable:

- If you plan to speak from a script, be sure to position it, so that you can hold your head up while speaking.
- Most audiotaped presentations will sound better if you deliver them while seated—as long as you speak into the mike and gesture appropriately.
- If you use a table, put your mike stand on a piece of foam rubber to dampen any extraneous sounds.
- Keep your tapes brief. Short tapes have more impact than longer ones.
- If you must deliver a long presentation on tape, make a clear break in content, and begin a new aspect of your topic every 15 minutes or less.
- When you present information on audiotape, you are working strictly with an auditory medium. Thus, your listeners will attune to your message more quickly if you allow auditory verbs to dominate your opening. Gradually shift to an abundance of visual verbs to engage them in that mode, then move toward action verbs in the kinesthetic, or tactile, mode. Audiotapes differ in this respect from live presentations: For tape listeners your first mode of choice should be auditory; when audience members are physically present, you should emphasize the visual mode first.

TIPS FOR APPEARING ON VIDEOTAPE
Videotape is a flat, two-dimensional medium that conveys its own air of intimacy. These tips will help you make the best of your videotaped presentations:

- Look at the camera as though you were looking directly through to your audience. In your mind's eye, speak to an individual, rather than a group.
- Be sure your eye contact is at its best when you are making important points.

- If you work from cue cards, be sure they are where you can see them and still look directly into the camera.
- If you deliver your script from a teleprompter, it will probably be positioned in front of the camera lens, so that you will appear to be looking directly at the audience. You are in charge of the rate of speed at which your copy passes through the prompter. Speak at your own rate. With a prompter, there is a tendency to lapse into reading, rather than delivering. Be especially alert to maintaining your dynamics.
- When you are being taped by more than one camera, practice taking your cues from your floor director—the person who will tell you which camera to look at next.
- Consider what you will do with material you want to show your viewers. Generally, it is best to deliver your presentation as though you were giving it live—slides, overheads, flip charts, and all. Then, in the editing process, retain the vocal or narrative portion of your presentation, but have the visuals created electronically and dubbed into the final tape.

ADVANTAGES TO BOTH

Whether you present on audiotape or videotape, both offer one distinct advantage over live presentations: You can deliver part of your presentation, pause, collect your thoughts, and continue—as often as you like. You can also do retakes if you don't like something you have said.

Once you get used to the idea that you don't have a live audience to give you immediate feedback for your audiotaped and videotaped presentations, but that just about everything else remains the same, you will learn to be comfortable with these kinds of presentations, as well as with the live ones. They can be an important adjunct to your total communications program.

21
Before and After You Speak

Any speaking engagement is only as effective as the results it produces. The outcome is all-important. Achieving that outcome begins with the quality of the arrangements you make with the organization that will host your presentation, and ends only when you have gained all the appropriate extra mileage you can from your speaking engagement.

You have put your best effort into preparing your speech. Now you want people to hear it. Clients tell me that many host organizations are surprisingly uncreative when it comes to informing potential audience members about a forthcoming program that could interest them.

People charged with the responsibility leave town. They get saddled with other work. They wait too long. They assume "everyone" already knows. They feel that an announcement at a meeting a month ago (which few may have attended) will suffice. They fail to realize that even the best speaker can't attract an audience unless potential participants know that he or she is scheduled to appear. Even then, they have to learn this well enough in advance to plan their own schedules accordingly.

You can take specific steps to create advance publicity and build attendance through news releases, flyers, and other promotional devices.

Advance Publicity

Ask your contact with the host organization whether the group would mind your issuing advance news releases and inviting editors to attend. If you have a public relations department or agency to assist you, they will know what to do. If you have to go it alone, here are some steps that will help.

NEWS RELEASES

To gain all the mileage possible from your next presentation, issue a news release that announces your upcoming talk about three weeks in advance to the local media. Check the editorial deadlines for the trade press. They may need your announcement several weeks, or even months, ahead of the date. If appropriate, you should enclose a brief letter inviting each editor to cover your presentation.

Your news release should include your name, title, organization, the name of the host organization, the date, the time, the place, the occasion, and your topic. If your talk will be unusual in any way, say so in the news release. Keep the release to a single page, double-spaced, and be sure to include a phone number where you can be contacted. Let editors know whether you will be available for interviews before or after your talk.

You might also want to consider sending advance copies of your text—or at least significant excerpts—to the news media with the release. If relevant, you might also include a photograph and a brief biographical sketch.

Building Attendance

You want people to attend your program, and if people knew about it, many would probably want to attend. Here are some specific ways to help that happen.

MEETING NOTICES

They are essential, although they are notoriously frail in their ability to build up an attendance for anything. More often than not, they get tossed with the junk mail, or buried with the stuff that the recipient says he or she will look at "later." I myself just found such a notice: The event was held two months ago, and I had really wanted to attend.

You must do what you can to ensure that the notice that announces your speaking engagement stands out from the routine, month-in-month-out flyers that your potential attendees may receive from this organization. In fact, ask your host to send you samples of the last three or four meeting announcements. If they look like carbon copies with minor alterations, assert yourself, and offer to prepare your own. Then design—and print—one that will catch the reader's eye.

Make sure your flyer covers everything that is in your news release—and more. It should also appeal to the recipients' enlightened self-interest. It should tell them what's in it for them if they attend. It should cover the significance of your topic. Make it relevant to their needs and interests. Show how it differs from the usual "ho-hum" presentations they have heard on the same or similar topics.

Let them know why you are the right person to convey this information. Give them just enough of your credentials to get them thinking. Tell them something about your approach to the topic. Will you be informative, motivational, philosophical? Do you involve your audience members in special ways? What have others said about you?

Be sure that your announcement notes any departures from the routine of this organization. If your potential audience members are accustomed to meeting every Thursday at noon, and you are scheduled to talk on Tuesday at 7:00 P.M., you can be sure that some will show up two days late and wonder for all the world what happened. Give the same attention to unusual locations, as well.

PHONE CALLS

Ask whether the host organization will do a telephone canvass of its members, and whether they have a calling chain through which this could be done efficiently. It may be worth your time to encourage the chairperson to develop one if it does not already exist. Your rationale might be that while it may take a little longer the first time, it will then be in place for future meetings. Your gain will be a greater potential attendance. At least people will have heard about you.

FOLLOW-UP MAILINGS

Ask them whether they will (not *plan* to) send out follow-up notices. Three mailings spaced over four to six weeks will catch far more potential audience members than a single mailing ever will. Send at least one copy to home addresses. Mail received there has a more personal connotation. Make each mailing slightly different, if only in layout, to attract more attention.

Include a cover letter (or even a handwritten sentence or two on the flyer). The note might come from you, or the president of the host organization, or someone whose name will add impact to the mailing. Give recipients a way to respond. Whom should they call to register?

How do they mail in their payment? Has the organization provided a self-addressed envelope?

SPECIAL LETTERS

If you want to attract others outside the host organization, you can follow all the suggestions provided. However, you should also get a letter to the presidents and secretaries of every organization whose members might be likely to attend. Enclose a sample flyer, and offer to produce as many copies for them as they might need. Encourage them to enclose it with their next two mailings. Get this package out at least three months in advance if you expect any real responses from your efforts.

SETTING ADMISSION PRICES

When your host organization sets the price of admission as part of the planning effort, deal yourself in on the discussions—especially if you have a product to sell, such as books or tapes. Your prime considerations should be these: Is the price low enough to be attractive, yet high enough to convey the value of your information? Would you be better off incorporating the price of one of your books or tapes into the admission fee? (Host organizations will generally prefer you to sell the books and tapes after your presentation. Most authors will tell you that doing it this way rarely sells as many books or tapes as you might hope to sell.)

DOOR PRIZES

Provide door prizes and enclose tickets as a means of admission. Frequently, host organizations will use the ticket numbers to raffle off one of my books or tapes. This ties in even more closely with the reason for my talk, and motivates those who already intend to register to take action—especially if a deadline is given.

Following Up Your Speech

After you speak, there are additional avenues for getting your message across to participants and to others with whom you might want to communicate the same points. Of course, all this should be checked with the host organization in case they have their own plans. However, most speakers discover that many host organizations lack the time, staff, and budget to follow up each speaker's presentation individually—especially at national or regional conferences. So, unless you are the keynoter, let the host organization know you are prepared and willing to handle your own follow-up publicity.

In fact, even if you are the keynoter, you may want to assert yourself and get them to agree that you will handle postpublicity yourself. It pays to take the initiative. What is the old saw about which road is paved with good intentions?

As soon as you have finished your final draft of the speech, write a standard news release that covers the salient points of your presentation. The news release should always answer the questions who, what, when, where, why, and how for the reader. Keep the news release to a single page and double space it. It should appear on a heading that enables editors to know who sent it out and how to contact someone for further information.

At the bottom of each news release, handwrite a note offering to make yourself available for interviews on your topic. If you can provide a full text or if you are prepared to develop feature articles from portions of it, put that in writing, too.

Unless your name and reputation, alone, are sufficient to entice editors to tell their audiences about your speech, you will need to include something from your talk that will attract their attention: Include the more interesting, informative, entertaining, or controversial quotes from your speech. These help to attract editors' attention and to ensure that their audiences will learn about your speech.

Send this information to the newspapers, radio, and television stations that serve the area where you will speak. Send a similar package to trade or other publications that might be interested in your topic, or which serve the interests of your audience.

Most of your extra mileage after a presentation will come from two sources: The trade press and people who "should" have attended, but did not, or were unable to, attend. Be certain to mail copies of your full text (and the news release), along with a brief cover letter, to the trade publications. Review a master list of potential attendees, and narrow it down to those whom you want to receive your message. Mail them the full package. Then, mail only the news release and cover letter to the rest. Offer to send the full text to those who request it after reading your letter.

Consider other avenues for broadening the reach of your message. Have you done everything you can do appropriately within your own organization? Would it be appropriate to send a mailing to your alma mater, or to civic and social organizations of which you are a member?

COMMUNICATIONS
P.O. Box 3119 • Warrenton, VA • 22186
(703) 349-1039

STEPHEN C. RAFE WILL ADDRESS
NATIONAL CONFERENCE OF THE
AMERICAN SOCIETY FOR TRAINING AND DEVELOPMENT

Stephen C. Rafe, APR, President of Starfire Enterprises and
Rapport Communications, Warrenton, VA, will conduct a workshop titled,
"Presenting with a Purpose," at the national conference of the American
Society for Training and Development in Boston, MA, on Sunday, June 4.
The conference runs from June 4 through 8.

Rafe is an internationally known spokesperson-counselor and
lecturer whose clients have included Johnson & Johnson during the
Tylenol crisis, AT&T during the divestiture, and President Reagan's
Committee on Strategic Forces for the MX Missile. He is the author of
"The Executive's Guide to Successful Presentations," and his
observations on communications subjects appear frequently in the
professional and trade press.

Active in volunteer work, Rafe is a member of the Board of
Directors of No Greater Love, an organization dedicated to the
children and families of Americans who have lost their lives, or their
freedom, while serving our country and is also a member of the public
relations committee for Ronald MacDonald House in Washington, D.C.

-- xxx --

(In a comparable vein, copies of the news release announcing this book were sent to organizations in which I am well-known for reasons having little to do with the subject of this book, per se.)

Helping Yourself Succeed

Speakers and chairpersons have a lot in common: Both want the event to succeed, and both want to help one another as much as possible without intruding on each other's time. Both also require certain information and materials of one another that will help to ensure that mutual success. Like any good relationship, the one between the speaker and the host organization requires an investment—of time, planning, and communication—by both of you.

Most good presenters do their homework and welcome all the input they can obtain from their hosts. Here is a checklist that will help you to obtain that input in a logical and systematic way and to ensure that nothing has been left to chance. (Naturally, you may not need the answers to every question for every speaking engagement, and, on occasion, you may need questions answered that are not listed here.)

Checklist

YOUR ORGANIZATION
- Send me background on your organization, its purpose, and some of its more interesting history.

THE AUDIENCE
- Describe your participants by profession, occupation, or job title.
- Profile a "typical" registrant (age/occupation/etc.).
- What does the audience know about my topic?
- How many people do you estimate will attend?

THE EVENT
- What is the theme of the meeting?
- What are the meeting's goals and objectives?
- Can you provide me with a sample printed program for recent comparable events that your organization has held?

SCHEDULING
- What are the meeting dates?
- On what date(s) would you like me to speak?
- At what time(s) do I start?
- How much time is allocated for my talk? For questions?

THE PRESENTATION
- What should my topic and theme be?
- Would you like to suggest a title for the talk?
- How would you like me to treat the topic?
- What points should I emphasize?
- What will the speakers who precede and follow me cover?
- What else might precede or follow my talk?
- What is my format (lecture, panel discussion, workshop, etc.)?
Please provide names, addresses, biographies, and other pertinent information about the others who will share the dais.

LOCATION
- Where will the meeting be held? Which restaurant, hotel, or conference facility?
- How do I get there?
- Can you send me a map of the area?

PHYSICAL ARRANGEMENTS
- How much flexibility do I have in arranging audience seating (horseshoe, theater-style, classroom, chevron, round table, etc.)?
- Will the size of the room be appropriate for the size of the group?
- What is the room's configuration?
- Will there be a platform? Where? How large?
- Can you provide a floor plan?
- Will there be a lectern (table or free standing)?
- What kind of microphone(s) will be provided (lavalier, clip-on, hand-held, fixed, cordless)?

AUDIOVISUAL EQUIPMENT
- Can you provide screens and projectors (overhead or slide)?
- What kinds of boards (blackboards, felt, cork, other) are provided?
- Can you provide video equipment (monitors, recorders, cameras, tripods, lights, etc.)?
- Will you provide writing implements (pens, chalk, markers, etc.)?

• Can you have miscellaneous items on hand (three-prong adapters, extension cords, spare bulbs, batteries, etc.)?

ACTIVITIES
• Will I be expected or invited to attend any special functions?
• What is the timetable and attire for these functions?
• Will I receive complimentary registrations?
• May I attend other programs on the agenda? Is there a fee for doing so?

PRINTED MATERIALS
• Do you need advance copies of speakers' presentations?
• Will you reproduce handouts if I send you masters?
• Should I bring my own handouts?
• Would you like me to send or bring along a one-page, double-spaced introduction with my name spelled phonetically?
• What are your deadlines?

SELLING TAPES
• Are you planning to tape speakers' presentations?
• Will you be selling these tapes to others?
• What are your plans?
• If I agree to be taped, what do you offer in return? Additional publicity? Royalties or a percentage of income from tape sales? Courtesy copies? Other?

AIDES
• Will someone:
   Meet me at either the airport or hotel?
   Ensure that the presentation room meets all requirements?
   Help me with last-minute needs in the meeting room?
   Introduce me?
   Assist latecomers with seating?
   Attend to audience members special needs?
   Help distribute handouts?
   Collect requests for special information?
   Distribute and collect evaluation sheets?
   Operate audiovisual equipment?
   Help me locate special functions?
   Transport me to my point of departure?

TRAVEL
- Are reduced rates available?
- Should I book my own flights or other arrangements?
- If I drive, will you provide travel directions?
- If I fly, how should I get from the airport to the meeting facility?

LODGING
- At which hotel should I stay? Should I stay in the hotel where the conference will be held, or nearby?
- Please provide a selection of hotels in various price ranges if I am to pay my own expenses.
- Will you preregister me at the hotel? If so, will you be able to take care of such special needs as a nonsmoking room, a room away from elevators and street noise, a room near the conference facility, and so on?

PUBLICITY
- Do you want or need photos? What are your requirements?
- Do you want a biography?
- Do you want the title and a description of my talk?
- Do you want a news release from me?
- How will you handle advance and follow-up publicity to your members?
- How will you handle this with the trade press?
- If you're not sending out news releases, may I do this?
- Will there be print, radio, or television coverage or interviews?

FINANCES
Will you pay for the following directly, send me payment in advance, or reimburse me when I submit vouchers after the event? Will I be expected to incur any or all of these costs without any form of reimbursement?
- Speaker's fees.
- Airline or train tickets.
- Other transportation.
- Hotel.
- Meals.
- Miscellaneous.

OTHER

As you get closer to the event date, please let me know:

- The name of the building in which I will speak.
- The floor and room number or name.
- The projected attendance.
- Whether dignitaries will attend. Include names, titles, and background as appropriate.
- Whether reporters or photographers have indicated plans to cover my presentation.
- Any other recent developments.
- For my records, and as a courtesy, please send me copies of all flyers, programs, and other printed materials you develop and in which I am mentioned. Also, please pass along copies of any significant articles that mention my participation.

Epilogue

No matter how well you present information to audiences, you can always learn more about the process. Whether we consider making presentations an art, a craft, a skill, or a science, it is a process that allows room for improvement.

On the theory that successful people are always searching for new ways to become even better, you might want to continue your search beyond this book. Examine the reading list provided, and read one book at a time, starting with the one that attracts you most. Then, when you read that book, examine its bibliography for others of related interest, and continue the pursuit.

Read good speeches. Subscribe to newsletters that will keep you abreast of the latest presentation techniques and of significant speeches that have been delivered recently.

Look for role models. Observe those individuals in your professional and civic activities whose skills appeal to you. When you attend conferences, study speakers' techniques, setting content aside. Attend seminars on effective presentations. Become involved with organizations whose members practice their speaking skills, such as Toastmasters and the Jaycees.

Seek every opportunity to practice, one step at a time. Each time you specifically intend to use a new skill, begin by testing it in a low-stress, nonthreatening environment. Many community organizations look for speakers with an area of expertise that might interest their members. Start at the local level, with forgiving audiences, as you set your sights on your ultimate target.

Do this often, and with each step you take, you will find yourself rapidly developing presentation skills that will serve you well throughout your life.

Reading List

I hope you've enjoyed reading this book and that you will pursue other sources of information that will help you continue to improve your presentation skills. I developed this reading list from a review of the titles on business presentations, public speaking, writing, psychology, and behavior that I felt would help you most.

By no means is it exhaustive or exclusive. Many other fine books are in print on these subjects, and new ones come out all the time. Several of the books listed here contain useful bibliographies, and those resources can provide even more information in a given subject area. Your library can help you with further research into any of these areas.

Presenting Information

Abelson, Herbert, and Marvin Karlans. *Persuasion*. New York, Springer Publications Co., 1970.

Bernhard, Edgar. *Speakers on the Spot*. West Nyack, NY, Parker Publishing Co., 1977.

Bowling, Evelyn Burge. *Voice Power*. Harrisburg, PA, Stackpole Books, 1980.

Detz, Joan. *How to Write and Give a Speech*. New York, St. Martin's Press, 1984.

Douglass, Paul. *The Group Workshop Way in the Church*. New York, Association Press, 1956.

Frank, Milo. *How to Get Your Point Across in 30 Seconds or Less*. New York, Simon & Schuster, 1986.

Gard, Grant G. *The Art of Confident Speaking*. Englewood Cliffs, NJ, Prentice-Hall, 1986.

Greene, Alan. *The New Voice—How to Sing and Speak Properly*. Milwaukee, WI, Hal Leonard Publishing Corporation, n.d.

Jeffries, James R., and Jefferson D. Bates. *The Executive's Guide to Meetings, Conferences, & Audiovisual Presentations.* New York, McGraw-Hill, 1986.

Kenney, Michael. *Presenting Yourself.* New York, John Wiley & Sons, 1982.

Lobinger, John, Jr. *Business Meetings That Make Business.* New York, Collier Books, 1969.

McCullough, William J. *Hold Your Audience: The Successful Way to Public Speaking.* Englewood Cliffs, NJ, Prentice-Hall, 1978.

McFarland, Kenneth. *Eloquence in Public Speaking.* Englewood Cliffs, NJ, Prentice-Hall, 1961.

Miller, Sherod, Daniel Wackman, Elam Nunnally, and Carol Saline. *Straight Talk.* Rawson, NY, Wade Publishers, Inc., 1981.

Pendleton, Winston K. *Speaker's Handbook of Successful Openers and Closers.* Englewood Cliffs, NJ, Prentice-Hall, 1984.

Tarver, Jerry. *The Corporate Speech Writer's Handbook—A Guide for Professionals in Business, Agencies, and the Public Sector.* Westport, CT, Quorum Books, 1987.

Walters, Dorothy M. *The Great Communicators.* Glendora, CA, Royal Publishing Company, 1985.

Wilder, Lilyan. *Professionally Speaking.* New York, Simon & Schuster, 1986.

Managing Stress

Benson, Herbert. *The Relaxation Response.* New York, Avon Books, 1975.

Fensterheim, Herbert, and Jean Baer. *Stop Running Scared.* New York, Rawson Associates Publishers, 1977.

Green, Elmer, and Alyce Green. *Beyond Biofeedback.* New York, Dell Publishing, 1977.

Mann, Stanley. *Triggers—A New Approach to Self-Motivation.* Englewood Cliffs, NJ, Prentice-Hall, 1987.

McKay, Matthew, and Patrick Fanning. *Self-Esteem.* Oakland, CA, New Harbinger Publications, 1987.

Parks, Richard. *How to . . . Overcome Stage Fright.* Fremont, CA, F-P Press, 1979.

Robbins, Anthony. *Unlimited Power.* New York, Fawcett Columbine, 1986.

Tanner, Ogden. *Stress.* New York, Time-Life Books, 1976.

Humor

Bassingdale, Bob. *How Speakers Make People Laugh.* West Nyack, NY, Parker Publishing Co., 1976.

Blakely, Dock, Joe Griffith, Robert Henry, and Jeanne Robertson. *How the*

Platform Professionals Keep Them Laughing. Wharton, TX, Rich Publishing Co., 1987.

Blumenfeld, Esther, and Lynne Alpren. *The Smile Connection.* Englewood Cliffs, NJ, Spectrum Books/Prentice-Hall, 1985.

Brings, Lawrence M. *Clever Introductions for Chairmen.* Minneapolis, MN, T. S. Denison & Co., 1956.

Iapoce, Michael. *A Funny Thing Happened on the Way to the Boardroom— Using Humor in Business Speaking.* New York, John Wiley & Sons, 1988.

Perret, Gene. *How to Hold Your Audience with Humor.* San Bernardino, CA, Borgo Press, 1989.

Communication and Behavior

Birren, Faber. *Color and Human Response.* New York, Van Nostrand, Reinhold, 1978.

Bolton, Robert. *People Skills.* Englewood Cliffs, NJ, Prentice-Hall, 1979.

Bristol, Claude M. *The Magic of Believing.* New York, Pocket Books, 1948.

Campbell, David. *If You Don't Know Where You're Going, You'll Probably End Up Somewhere Else.* Niles, IL, Argus Communications, 1974.

Korda, Michael. *Power.* New York, Ballantine Books, 1975.

LaHaye, Tim. *Your Temperament: Discover Its Potential.* Wheaton, IL, Tyndale House, 1984.

Malloy, John T. *Dress for Success.* New York, Warner Books, 1975.

Maslow, Abraham. *Motivation and Personality.* New York, Harper & Row, 1954.

Miller, G. A. "The Magical Seven, Plus or Minus Two: Some Limits on Our Capacity for Processing Information," *Psychological Review* (1956), 63: 81–97.

Nierenberg, Gerald I., and Henry H. Calero. *Meta-Talk.* New York, Simon & Schuster, 1973.

Sutphen, Richard. "Battle for Your Mind" (audiocassette). Malibu, CA, Valley of the Sun Publishing, 1984.

Thompson, David S. *Language.* New York, Time-Life Books, 1975.

Weintraub, Walter. *Verbal Behavior, Adaptation and Psychopathology.* New York, Springer, 1981.

Non-verbal Communication

Ekman, Paul. *Telling Lies.* New York, Berkley Books, 1985.

Ekman, P., W. V. Friesen, and P. Ellsworth. *Emotion in the Human Face.* New York, Pergamon Press, 1972.

Fast, Julian. *Body Language*. New York, Pocket Books, 1971.
Morris, Desmond. *Manwatching*. New York, Harry N. Abrams, 1977.
Nierenberg, Gerald I., and Henry H. Calero. *How to Read a Person Like a Book*. New York, Pocket Books, 1971.
Whiteside, Robert L. *Face Language*. New York, Pocket Books, 1974.

Marketing and Sales Communication

Moine, Donald J., and John H. Herd. *Modern Persuasion Strategies*. Englewood Cliffs, NJ, Prentice-Hall, 1984.
Rein, Irving, Philip Kotler, and Martin Stoller. *High Visibility*. New York, Dodd, Mead & Co., 1987.
Zunin, Leonard, and Natalie Zunin. *Contact: The First Four Minutes*. New York, Ballantine Books, 1972.

Negotiating

Cohen, Herb. *You Can Negotiate Anything*. New York, Bantam Books, 1980.
Elgin, Suzette Haden. *The Gentle Art of Verbal Self-Defense*. Englewood Cliffs, NJ, Prentice-Hall, 1980.
Goffman, Erving. *Relations in Public*. London, Penguin, 1971.
Nierenberg, Gerald I. *The Art of Negotiating*. New York, Simon & Schuster, 1981.

Writing

Flesch, Rudolph. *The ABC of Style*. New York, Harper & Row, 1964.
Hayakawa, S. I. *The Use and Misuse of Language*. Greenwich, CT, Fawcett Publications, Inc., 1979.
McCarthy, Edward H. *Speechwriting—A Professional Step-by-Step Guide for Executives*. Dayton, OH, The Executive Speaker Co., 1989.
Strunk, William, Jr., and E. B. White. *The Elements of Style*. New York, Macmillan, 1959.
Welsh, James J. *The Speech Writing Guide*. New York, John Wiley & Sons, 1968.

Newsletters and Periodicals

"Boardroom Reports." 330 W. 42nd St., New York, NY 10036.
"Communication Briefings." 140 S. Broadway, Pitman, NJ 08071.

"Current Comedy." Comedy Center, P.O. Box 1992, Wilmington, DE 19899.

"The Executive Speaker." P.O. Box 292437, Dayton, OH 45429.

"The Humor Project." Joel Goodman, Saratoga Institute, 110 Spring St., Saratoga Springs, NY 12866.

"The Jokesmith." Edward C. McManus, editor. 44 Queen's View Rd., Marlborough, MA 01752.

The Journal of Business Communication. Box 8334, College of Business Administration, Abilene Christian University, Abilene, TX 79699.

"Sharing Ideas Among Professional Speakers." P.O. Box 1120 Glendora, CA 91740.

"Soundings." Art Lenehan, 12 Daniel Road, Fairfield, NJ 07006.

"Speaker's Digest." Box 363, Salisbury, CT 06068.

"Speechwriter's Weekly." 407 S. Dearborn St., Suite 1360, Chicago, IL 60605.

"Toastmaster." 2200 North Grand Ave., Santa Ana CA, 92711.

Organizations and Workshops

Association for Business Communication. University of Illinois, 608 S. Wright St., Urbana, IL 61901

"Humor & Creativity: Personal & Professional Skillshop." Joel Goodman. Saratoga Institute, 110 Spring St., Saratoga Springs, NY 12866.

International Communications Industries Association. 3150 Spring St., Fairfax, VA 22031.

"The International Humor Conference." Margaret Baker. English Dept., Brigham Young University—Hawaii, Box 1904, Laie, HI 96762–1294.

National Forensic Association. Dept. of Communication and Theater Arts, 165 Fine Arts, University of Wisconsin, Eau Claire, WI 54701.

National Speakers Association. 4747 North Seventh St. Suite 310, Phoenix AZ 85014.

Speech Communication Association. 5105 Blacklick Rd., Building E, Annandale, VA 22003.

Toastmasters International. 2200 North Grand Ave., Santa Ana, CA 92711.

"Speak-Up Jaycee" Program, United States Jaycees. P.O. Box 7, Tulsa, OK 74121–0007.

Academic Journals

Several cover current research in the fields of behavior, communications, psychology, and related areas of interest. Check your local university's library for information on these publications and others:

Psychological Reports

The Journal of Psychology

Psychological Record
Journal of Personality and Social Psychology
The Journal of Communication
Speech Monographs
Journal of Personality
Canadian Journal of Behavioral Science

Neuro-linguistic Programming

Techniques used in the field of neuro-linguistics have been incorporated in this book. The following is a partial list of the publications available in this field:

Bandler, Richard. *Magic in Action.* Cupertino, CA, Meta Publications, 1985.

Bandler, Richard, and John Grinder. *Reframing.* Moab, UT, Real People Press, 1982.

Bandler, Richard, and Grinder, John. *Frogs into Princes.* Moab, UT, Real People Press, 1979.

Bandler, Richard, and Grinder, John. *The Structure of Magic I.* Moab, UT, Real People Press, 1975.

Cameron-Bandler, Leslie. *They Lived Happily Ever After.* Cupertino, CA, Meta Publications, 1978.

Dilts, Robert B., John Grinder, Richard Bandler, Judith DeLozier, and Leslie Cameron-Bandler. *Neuro-Linguistic Programming I.* Cupertino, CA, Meta Publications, 1979.

Dilts, Robert. *Roots of Neuro-Linguistic Programming.* Cupertino, CA, Meta Publications, 1983.

Dilts, Robert. *Applications of Neuro-Linguistic Programming.* Cupertino, CA, Meta Publications, 1983.

Gordon, David. *Therapeutic Metaphors.* Cupertino, CA, Meta Publications, 1978.

Grinder, John, and Richard Bandler. *The Structure of Magic II.* Cupertino, CA, Science and Behavior Books, 1976.

Grinder, John, and Richard Bandler. *Trance-Formations.* Moab, UT, Real People Press, 1981.

Jacobson, Sid. *Meta-cation: Prescriptions for Some Ailing Educational Processes.* Cupertino, CA, Meta Publications, 1983.

Robbins, Anthony. *Unlimited Power.* New York, Fawcett Columbine, 1986.

Yeager, Joseph. *Thinking about Thinking with NLP.* Cupertino, CA, Meta Publications, 1985.

Yeager, Joseph. *A Collection of Articles on Management and NLP, Fourth Edition.* Newtown, PA, Eastern NLP Institute, 1985.

Index

Rapport Communications prepares people at all levels in all fields to present information and respond to questions. Our methods help people make their points, achieve win-win outcomes, and gain audience acceptance in any situation—even under stress and regardless of the personalities involved.

Our seminars carry familiar titles:

Presentations: public speaking, sales presentations, videotaped appearances, government testimony, management presentations, serving as "talent" on radio or television commercials (or PSAs), editorial board briefings, and financial presentations (especially meetings of shareholders or security analysts).

Writing: speechwriting for professionals, speechwriting for non-professionals, and feature articles writing.

Interviews: talk shows, crisis response, radio and television interviews, and executive employment interviews.

Each program is custom-designed from a list of approximately 200 instructional units which you select, according to the priorities you assign. The issues and content you specify are used throughout. Thus, each program fulfills your expectations. Participants learn new information rapidly, retain it well, and recall it when they need it most.

For a free list of Rapport seminars available to the public in your area, drop us a note. I would be pleased to show you how our services can provide better skills for you or members of your organization.

Stephen C. Rafe, APR, *President*
Rapport Communications
Dept. HRB P.O. Box 3119
Warrenton, VA 22186
(703) 349-1039